The Latina|o Theatre Commons 2013 National Convening
A Narrative Report

By Brian Eugenio Herrera

Edited by Jayne Benjulian and Jamie Gahlon

A PUBLICATION OF HOWLROUND

A COMMONS BY AND FOR PEOPLE WHO MAKE PERFORMANCE

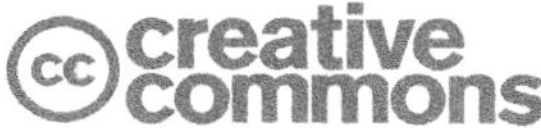

ISBN: 978-1-939006-04-2 (paperback)
ISBN: 978-1-939006-05-9 (e-book)
Library of Congress Control Number: 2014958227

Center for the Theater Commons/HowlRound.com
Emerson College, c/o Office of the Arts
120 Boylston Street
Boston, MA 02116
USA

For inquiries, e-mail editor@howlround.com or call +1 617-824-3017

Printed in the United States of America

Book Design: Michael Quanci quancidesign.com
Cover Image: Lucy Gram

TABLE OF CONTENTS

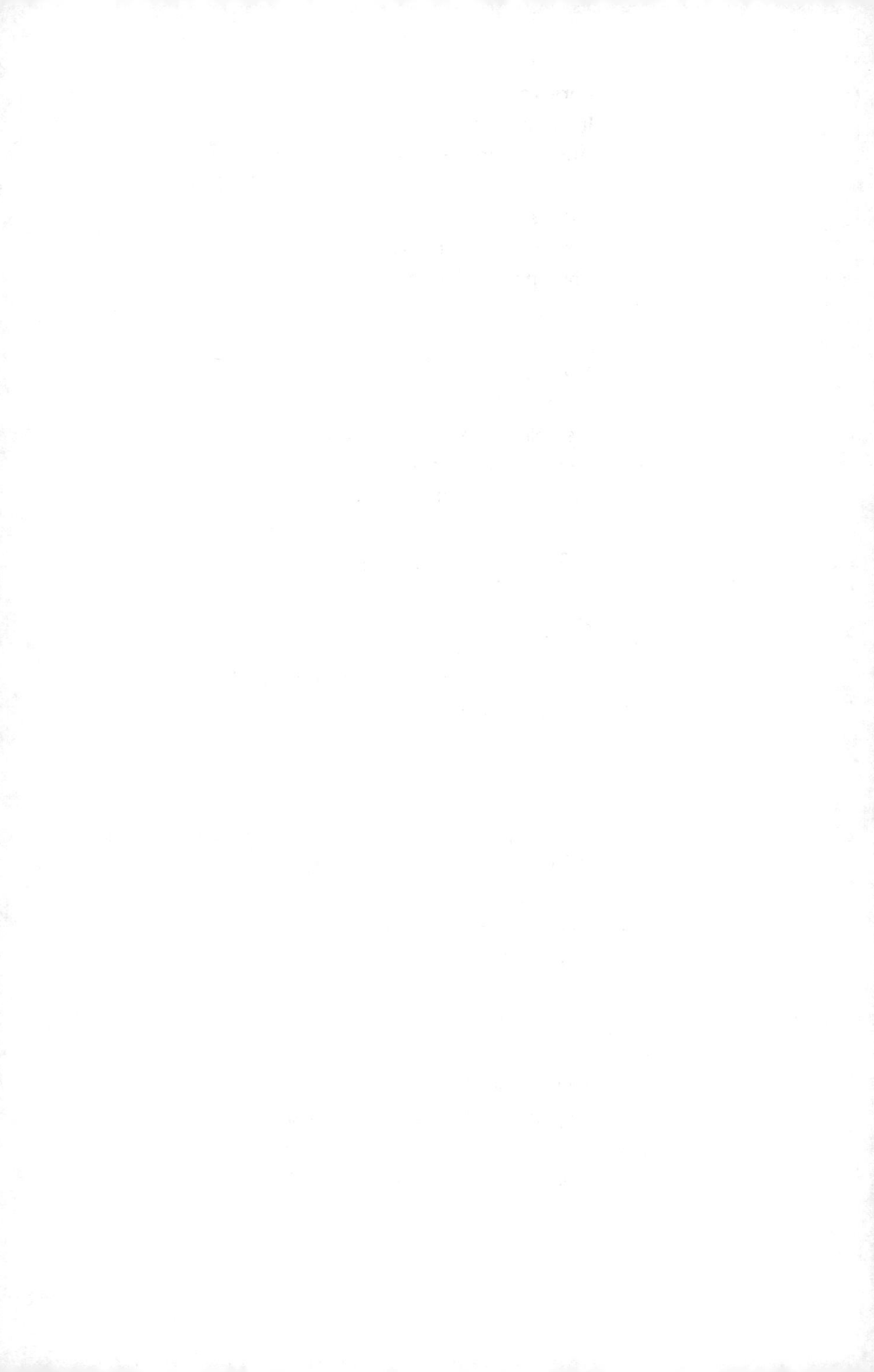

Karen Zacarías

It was time for Latina/o artists to discuss and design a viable, energetic, sustainable, inclusive "something" that would serve a wide band of Latina/o artists nationally.

IN MAY OF 2012, under the auspices of my residency with the American Voices New Play Institute and HowlRound at Arena Stage, I convened a small group of geographically diverse and mostly independent Latina/o artists to talk candidly at *calzón quitado* about the challenges and the hopes of being a theater artist in this country. A series of national events, some in my hometown of Washington D.C., had galvanized several Latina/o artists to organize and speak out over the Internet. I realized that many of my virtual *compadres* and *comadres* had never been in one room altogether. I didn't want the energy to fade, because it was energy at the most important level: the grassroots. My instinct was that it was time for Latina/o artists to discuss and design a viable, energetic, sustainable, inclusive "something" that would serve a wide band of Latina/o artists nationally.

Eight of us showed up. Many of us did not know each other. There were sandwiches, but we had no formal agenda. As the day progressed, and we ate, and shared, and dreamed, every one of the participants expressed a deep desire to bring together a larger group of artists to form a concrete action plan. We knew from past experiences that the group had to be large enough to include a variety of perspectives, but small enough to be responsive and effective in building a solid platform for something larger.

The candid discussion moved into a consensus and plan for sustainable action. Our hopes and dreams embrace the recognition of a canon of Latina/o drama; an ongoing national and regional arena for conversation live and online; and the production of more powerful, diverse Latina/o voices in the American Theater.

HowlRound, now based at Emerson College's Office of the Arts, agreed to serve as our fiscal and organizational agent during this phase. We were all aware that this would involve a strong work commitment from a small planning committee and that we would need the advice and support of a Steering Committee. Thus began the foundation and the fundraising for the Latina/o Theatre Commons (LTC): a fluid national platform that serves and connects diverse Latina/o theater artists throughout the United States.

The original eight reached out to more than a dozen key members of the Latina/o theater community and formed a diverse Steering Committee of experienced, nationally recognized leaders. Together, the twenty-five became the LTC. The first item on the agenda: organize a national meeting to connect the many vibrant conversations happening all over the nation and set the stage for what Latina/o artists want and need in the American Theater.

The first conference of the LTC was held in Boston in October of 2013. It was the largest reunion of Latina/o artists in over twenty-five years. At that meeting the almost eighty delegates and several dozen online participants in five different cities discussed, shared, and dreamed.

Together, these representatives plus their delegations from home became the LTC. The conference was unique; the results, as you will read here, are inspiring.

At its core, the LTC is about taking sustainable dramatic "action."

There are two ideas behind the LTC: first, its growth is concentric, like the trunk of a strong oak that grows systematically wider and deeper with each iteration; second, the goal is to have a diverse band of regional representatives—large enough to spread the work, but small enough for each member to be accountable and effective. Our mission is to listen to each other, find common goals, and pursue our shared dreams with equanimity, transparency, and purpose.

At the 2013 conference, the LTC created an ambitious national agenda. The only way to sustain our momentum is to work in waves: with members sprinting and passing the baton as they complete projects and conceive new ideas. We are a collective; everybody on board is a busy individual; one person need not shoulder the organization; participation is fluid and flexible, but participation and accountability are key. We work as a collective, each one of us doing a small part, with the belief and knowledge that large changes can and will happen if we capitalize on the values of inclusivity, sustainability, creativity, transparency, and momentum.

We are all artists, scholars, producers. At its core, the LTC is about taking sustainable dramatic "action." At the end of the day, our purpose is to provide different modes of connectivity, support, and inspiration to help us *all* (not just artists of Latina/o heritage) grow and deepen individually and collectively as theater artists.

¡Bienvenidos todos!

Karen Zacarías
Playwright

Anne García-Romero

INTRODUCTION

IN MARCH 2013, the Latina/o Theatre Commons (LTC) held a meeting of our newly formed Steering Committee in Boston, hosted by HowlRound, with support from The Andrew W. Mellon Foundation. We'd received a grant from the Doris Duke Charitable Foundation to fund our Fall 2013 Convening. Our Steering Committee of twenty-five Latina/o theater artists and scholars met for two days on the campus of Emerson College to brainstorm, plan, discuss, strategize, and continue to expand our circle. We formed three sub-committees: Programming, Outreach, and Fundraising and began to plan our Convening in earnest. We forged ahead with the continuing guidance of HowlRound and the considerable expertise of Jamie Gahlon, HowlRound's Associate Director.

Clyde Valentín, Former Executive Director of the New York City-Based Hip-Hop Theater Festival and newly appointed to the Southern Methodist University's Meadows School of the Arts Staff in Dallas, TX, chaired our Outreach sub-committee. Clyde contributed his substantial experience as an arts organizer and innovator to galvanize our outreach efforts. This initial Convening could only include around seventy-five participants, due to our funding parameters, as our budget covered travel, lodging, and meals for each participant. We wanted the widest range of participation possible with diverse representation of gender, artistic discipline, region, and career stage. Our entire Steering Committee recommended individuals, and we began the process of inviting Convening participants. While we could only include a limited number, we worked to establish satellite sites in Chicago, Dallas, Los Angeles, Miami, and New York City, where other people might participate in the Convening via Skype conferencing, and we engaged HowlRound TV to livestream most of the events. We also hired an official Convening Tweeter and Blogger. In preparation for the Convening, our Outreach sub-committee created a series of surveys in which participants provided reflections on the state of the field. The Outreach sub-committee included Christopher Acebo, Jacob Padrón, Richard Perez, Tlaloc Rivas, Anthony Rodriguez, Olga Sanchez, Patricia Ybarra, and Karen Zacarías.

Kinan Valdez, Artistic Director of El Teatro Campesino in San Juan Bautista, California, chaired our Programming sub-committee. Kinan had spent the previous two years traveling across the country, connecting with Latina/o theater artists who have organized coalitions in Dallas, Los Angeles, Miami, New York City, and Oregon. Kinan shared his considerable knowledge of the Latina/o theater field and his expertise as an Artistic Director to envision and shape our programming for the Convening. A plan began to emerge using the frame of the four directions (North, South, East, and West) as a gathering point, leading into a series of listening circles comprised of the various artistic disciplines, and ending with sessions to craft strategies, concrete actions, and goals that further the growth of Latina/o theater. To support the development of the program, we engaged Dr. Roberto Vargas, a group facilitation expert, to consult and share best practices with Kinan, Juliette Carrillo, and Dr. Jorge Huerta. With this training, Kinan and his sub-committee created a program that honored our past, engaged our present, and envisioned our future. Sub-committee members included Luis Alfaro, Juliette Carrillo, Dr. Jorge Huerta, Tlaloc Rivas, Diane Rodriguez, Olga Sanchez, Clyde Valentín, and Karen Zacarías.

I served as our Fundraising sub-committee chair, collaborating with members Abel López, Associate Artistic Director of Gala Hispanic Theater, Lisa Portes, Head of MFA Directing at DePaul University, and José Luis Valenzuela, Artistic Director of the Los Angeles Theatre Center. We focused our efforts on five funding areas: national, corporate, regional,

> The LTC emphasizes horizontal empowerment and engagement. Our work highlights the importance of honoring the individual and collective voices in the Latina/o theater community.

individual, and academic. Our Duke Foundation grant stipulated that we match a percentage of our award. We applied to a variety of funding sources, with additional grant writing assistance from Tlaloc Rivas and Karen Zacarías. While fundraising for a new initiative with no previous track record had its challenges, we began to make contacts and receive funding from national and regional organizations as well as individual donors. Many of our Convening participants work in academia, and their institutions were able to support our efforts. We completed our match by the time the Convening began on October 31, 2014.

Tlaloc Rivas and I served also as co-chairs of the LTC Steering

Committee. Using the online Basecamp project management platform, the Steering Committee worked together to share information. Through monthly, bi-monthly, and weekly conference calls Tlaloc and I moderated, the LTC members continued to work in earnest. We held over fifty conference calls in which we discussed, planned, shared, dreamed, and forged ahead together to realize our Convening. The LTC Steering Committee members are all volunteers. During those months, our Steering Committee members had also been writing, designing, directing, and producing plays in Ashland, Chicago, Iowa City, Los Angeles, New York City, Norway, San Juan Bautista, and Washington D.C. We'd been teaching classes and engaging in scholarship at institutions such as Brown, DePaul University, Princeton, UCLA, University of Iowa, and the University of Notre Dame. Thus, with our very active professional lives, I was continually struck by our members' spirit of generosity, endless hard work, visionary leadership, commitment to service, and passion for the field of Latina/o theater.

The LTC emphasizes horizontal empowerment and engagement. Our work highlights the importance of honoring the individual and collective voices in the Latina/o theater community. I'm grateful for all the remarkable work that our Steering Committee has accomplished thus far. I've been honored by the opportunity to serve with this outstanding group of theater artists and scholars. Our Convening in Boston was the beginning of many more expansive conversations and connections that continue to advance the field of Latina/o theater in the twenty-first century.

Adelante! Sí se puede!

Anne García-Romero
Playwright and Scholar
Assistant Professor of Theater, University of Notre Dame

In this book, I approach the Convening as a performance event, or an experience in the shared space of lived time, and document it as such.

THIS BOOK OFFERS a detailed narrative account of what happened at the 2013 Latina/o Theatre Commons (LTC) National Convening. Commissioned at the request of both HowlRound: A Center for the Theater Commons at Emerson College and the Steering Committee of the LTC, this work departs—in style, scope, and scale—from the conventions of a "report" typically submitted to funders and other sponsoring entities after such an event. In this book, I approach the convening as a performance event, or an experience in the shared space of lived time, and document it as such. What follows, then, is neither an abstract summary nor a personal reflection; nor is it a direct transcription of events. Because I am a historian by training, inclination, and profession, I do not write this account as a journalist, ethnographer, or critic. Instead, I write it as a historian might—drawing from extant sources to compose a verifiably accurate account of what happened so that the reader might apprehend the significance of the events described.

I offer, then, a historical account of this very recent past, translating the 2013 Convening's archive into an accessible narrative, so that the event's significance might enter the historical record in ways of use and interest to students and practitioners of today and of tomorrow. As an exploration in writing what I have come to call "the history of our contemporary moment," this book also explores how an academic historian like myself might contribute to the urgent (and time sensitive) task of performance documentation outside the sometimes closed circuit (and glacial pace) of scholarly publication.

My sources for this account draw almost exclusively from documentations of the event available through the public record on Howl-Round (howlround.com). In particular, the archive of livestream video captured by Howl-Round TV (still accessible at howlround.tv) proved indispensable, with most quotations from participants being drawn from my own transcriptions of these recordings. For those sessions not captured on video, I was fortunate to have access to the expert notes taken by a team of Emerson College student note-takers. Real-time documentation of the Convening on a host of social media platforms (especially Facebook, Twitter, Instagram, and Storify), as well as the daily reports on HowlRound written by Srila Nayak, permitted invaluable additional views of the proceedings, both from those participants present in Boston and those observing virtually from afar. Likewise, written reflections by Convening participants—composed in prose, poetic, and dramatic form and submitted to me in the weeks immediately following the event—deepened my appreciation of the experience. My sincere thanks to Elisa Marina Alvarado, Rose Cano, Juliette Carrillo, Georgina H. Escobar, Micha Espinosa, Amparo Garcia-Crow, Ricardo Gutierrez, Jorge Huerta, Alberto Justiano, Josefina López, Tiffany Ana López, Sandra Marquez, Teresa Marrero, Matthew Paul Olmos, Anthony Rodriguez, Elaine Romero, Olga Sanchez, Caridad Svich, and Patricia Ybarra for sharing their reflections. Though only some of these reflections are cited within this text, each guided my work on this report in invaluable ways.

The task of composing this report far exceeded my expectations, and I know the scale and complexity of my first draft came as something of a shock to my HowlRound collaborators. I am thus especially grateful for the critical generosity, editorial acumen, and sheer stamina of Jayne Benjulian, Polly Carl, and Jamie Gahlon in bringing this work to press. Attentive readings by Anne García-Romero and Karen Zacarías contributed additional clarity. Working with designer Michael Quanci provided a welcome opportunity to amplify the report's readability. Even with all this expert help, however, the narrative—especially the inevitable errors, oversights, and gaps within it—are mine. (Indeed, the gaps within the extant documentation of this thoroughly documented event, in tandem with the limits of my own personal participation at the 2013 Convening, does mean that a full accounting of the Convening's rich "after hours" cultivation of creativity and community remains as yet unwritten.)

I am enduringly grateful for the opportunity to compose this report. Doing so permitted me to experience the 2013 LTC National Convening twice, first as participant, and later as author. Each experience reminded me not only of the formidable challenges facing Latina/o theatermakers today, but also of the defiant spirit, acuity, and commitment of Latina/o theater artists as they confront these obstacles and create worthy routes beyond them. Composing this report also confirmed my belief that perhaps the greatest resource we have as Latina/o theatermakers is the force of our collaboration. The Convening itself marks just such a collaboration—a historic gathering that invited Latina/o theatermakers to adopt critical stances of creative generosity with and for each other so that something unprecedented might manifest. I offer this account in the hope that its documentation of what happened in 2013 might serve as both touchstone and prompt for future collaborations instigated within the ongoing movement that is the LTC.

Brian Eugenio Herrera
Princeton, New Jersey

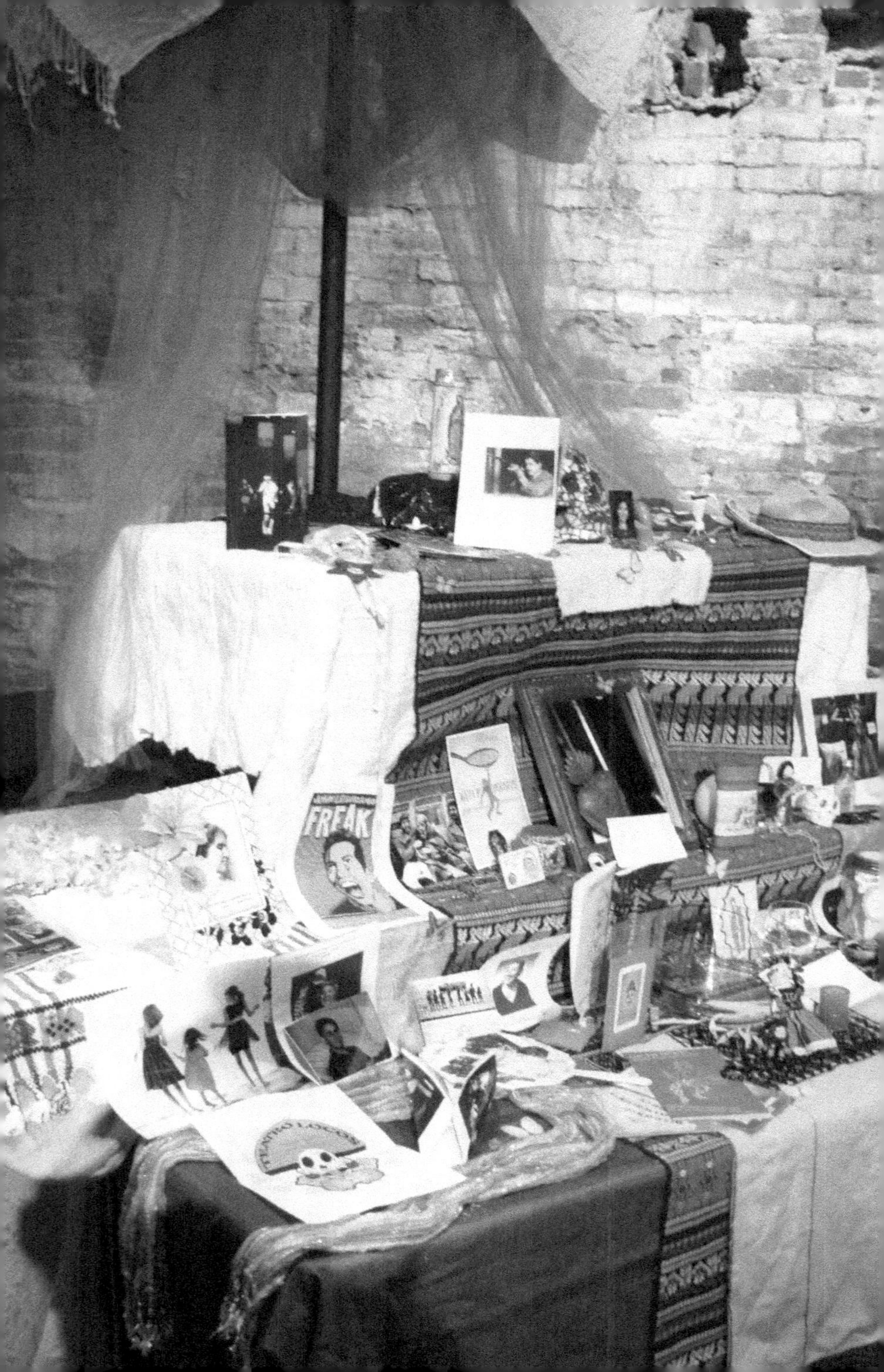

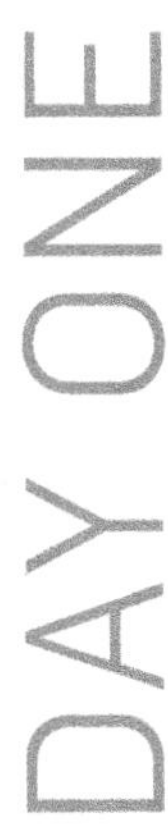

Thursday 31 October

"The family reunion has begun." —Luis Alfaro

Welcoming and Blessing

The Convening began in the evening on October 31, 2013. Nearly eighty Latina/o actors, playwrights, directors, designers, producers, and administrators representing not-for-profit, community-based, and academic theater organizations arrived from across the country. They were joined by a dozen or so HowlRound staff and volunteers. Assembled in the Jackie Liebergott Black Box Theatre at Emerson College's Paramount Center, these artists created the first Latina/o Theatre Commons (LTC) National Convening.

Olga Sanchez, the Artistic Director of Portland's Milagro Theatre and one of the event's three facilitators, invited all in the room to "take a breath together." Upon their collective exhale, Sanchez offered a prayerful invocation:

Sanchez offered a prayerful invocation:

In joy, in anticipation, in wonder, we are gathered in the name of art and community. We have journeyed to so many places in our lives and have arrived at this place, at this theater, at the same time.

We arrive as individuals but, in arriving, we have created something larger: a circle. A circle that reaches beyond these walls. To that which we thank, we humbly ask: Please help us to bring our communities into the circle with us, for we are ambassadors. We thank our circle for its embrace as we journey through the next few days together.

In joy, in anticipation, in wonder, we are gathered in the name of art and community. We have journeyed to so many places in our lives and have arrived at this place, at this theater, at the same time.

We arrive as individuals but, in arriving, we have created something larger: a circle. A circle that reaches beyond these walls. To that which we thank, we humbly ask: Please help us to bring our communities into the circle with us, for we are ambassadors. We thank our circle for its embrace as we journey through the next few days together.

Upon the conclusion of Sanchez's invocation, another of the event's co-facilitators Kinan Valdez, Producing Artistic Director of El Teatro Campesino in San Juan Batista, California, stepped forward and proclaimed: "Welcome, everybody, to the Latina/o Theatre Commons National Convening!" [*Cheers and applause*] This is a historic moment—the first national Convening of Latina/o theatermakers in over twenty-five years, the first of this century, and the first of this millennium."

> "The generosity of spirit is sending the room into another orbit."
> —Luis Alfaro

Valdez reaffirmed the Convening's guiding objective: "Over these three days, we will be weaving a beautiful narrative" by asking three guiding questions: Why are we here? How did we get here? Where are we going? "All of us in this particular room are here to serve as ambassadors." Although "there are numerous people who are not in this particular circle," Valdez reminded the group,

we [are] a cross-section of the Latina/o theater field…not a perfect cross-section but [this gathering] does speak to the state of our

The Six Stances

As adapted from Alan Briskin and the Collective Wisdom Initiative

1 Deep listening or opening with all one's critical and creative faculties to what is being expressed;

2 Suspension of certainty or an embrace of the risk of not already knowing the answer;

3 Seeking diverse perspectives or gathering and valuing perspectives from all those configuring the group;

4 Respect for others or cultivating a sense of mutual commitment to the common purpose of the group;

5 Welcoming all that arises or an embrace of both the unpleasant and pleasant emotions stirred by a gathering of this kind; and

6 Trust in the transcendent or an acceptance of the collective acuity that might manifest when a group of individuals comes together in common purpose.

current relationships. And we are hoping, though this three-day Convening, [to] build upon those relationships, strengthen them, and bring more people into this particular field. … We are going to spend three days cultivating, honoring, and reflecting upon the collective wisdom that we all carry with us.

Facilitator Kinan Valdez then introduced what he and his co-facilitators would come to call "our six stances," those principles of group collaboration that would provide a framework for the interactive inquiry staged by the Convening. Adopted and adapted from the ideas developed by Alan Briskin and the Collective Wisdom Initiative, paper printouts of these six stances circulated throughout the room as Valdez introduced each of them. Valdez invited the group "to show your commitment to this process, to us, and to you. Please raise your hand, an expression of your commitment to this group."

The third of the Convening's three facilitators Clyde Valentín, former Executive Director of the HI-ARTS Festival and current director of the Arts + Urbanism Initiative at Southern Methodist University, stepped forward to talk the participants through the agenda for the forthcoming three days. Valentín introduced the group to the variety of documentation strategies at work—HowlRound TV livestreaming, Emerson student note-takers, flipcams available for participant use—before inviting the members of the LTC Steering Committee to stand both in acknowledgment of their work in making the event happen and also to identify them as fellow stewards for the Convening's complex itinerary. Next, Valentín welcomed several guests to the microphone to speak about the genesis of the Convening, HowlRound and Emerson College's role in hosting the Convening, the notion of "a commons" as a coordinating premise, and the organizational apparatus of the Convening itself.

Up first, Karen Zacarías (former Playwright-in-Residence at Washington D.C.'s Arena Stage) offered a brief narrative account of the inspiration for both LTC and the Convening by reflecting on her family's parable of "the monkey with the green tail"—a tale of broken promises and unanticipated discoveries—as a metaphor for how the isolated struggles of U.S. Latina/o theatermakers become a source of power when they come together to talk. Zacarías recounted how eight diverse Latina/o theater artists from across the nation came together and, in the space of twenty-four hours, developed the plan that, seventeenth months later, manifested as this LTC National Convening.

Zacarías then welcomed Polly Carl, Director of HowlRound, to the microphone. Carl introduced the HowlRound staff and Emerson's Executive Director of the Office of Arts, Rob Orchard, who offered his own words of welcome before turning the microphone to Emerson's Chief Academic Officer Michaela Whalen to do the same. Then, Polly Carl offered her own welcome with some words about HowlRound and a theater commons.

"The impetus for HowlRound," Polly Carl explained, "comes from the idealistic notion that theater is for everyone. It comes in response to a prevailing sense of scarcity that can drive our behavior as a field and a firm belief that the scarcity mindset will only lead to more scarcity." Carl continued, "If you look around this room, what we see is abundance—an abundance of knowledge and resources just waiting to be released."

HowlRound designs and develops online knowledge platforms and in-person gatherings for the sake of fostering a theater commons to release our shared abundance and perpetuate the ideal that sharing abundance will make for a better and more accessible theater. The key words for HowlRound, Carl said, are: access, participation, self-determination, peer-to-peer learning and sharing, and the concept of moving from "I" to "we":

> *Many gatherings like this come together because a group of people are sitting in an organization and saying we should talk about diversity. So they decide to create a convening. It's a familiar kind of top-down approach where the institution drives the agenda, and where the problem is identified through the institution. But in the case of this gathering, something different has happened. Karen Zacarías approaches HowlRound to say "I'm troubled about the state of Latina/o theater artists in this country. Where do we come together? How do we empower ourselves?" She calls together a handful of people for a conversation that HowlRound hosts. That group self-determines and writes a grant to host a larger gathering. They get the grant. The group creates a Steering Committee. The Steering Committee creates an outline for a Convening and it identifies all of you as ambassadors to that Convening. But you represent cities all around the country. You represent your community and your community is yet another circle of engagement and participation. Five cities—Miami, Los Angeles, Dallas, New York, Chicago—will join us via Skype. We will livestream this entire convening. The "I" of Karen Zacarías becomes the "we" of a nation, and that's how a theater commons takes an idealistic notion and turns it into reality. HowlRound welcomes you to Boston!"*
> [Huge applause]

Carl welcomed Anne García-Romero and Tlaloc Rivas, the co-chairs of the Convening's Steering Committee. García-Romero and Rivas summarized the three prongs of their committee's work: Outreach (chaired by Clyde Valentín) oversaw the process of identifying and inviting participants, devising mechanisms to gather information from the field, and creating the satellite conversations across the country; Programming (chaired by Kinan Valdez) developed the structure, objectives, and itinerary for the Convening; and Fundraising (chaired by Anne García-Romero) sought funders at the national, regional, and institutional level. García-Romero and Rivas also noted the more recent establishment of a Documentation sub-committee responsible for developing mechanisms for the documentation and distribution of the work of the Convening in collaboration with HowlRound and other partners. "We're hopeful that the gathering here in Boston will be the start of many more expansive conversations and connections," Rivas and García-Romero concluded, "*Adelante! Sí se puede!*"

The Convening's facilitators returned to the microphone. Valdez reaffirmed, "Tonight is the night of connection, about knowing where we're coming from, quite literally…[and] also getting to know who is in the room."

"Tomorrow," said Sanchez," is about deepening our knowledge about what we do, how we do it, why we do it, what's up with what we do, what we love about what we do, [and] where we'd like to make improvements about how we do what we do."

"And, finally, Saturday," Valentín said, "We bring it home. We start to vision, to look forward, as we come up with some next steps. Are you ready?! *[Hoots and cheers]* Now we're going to create a circle!"

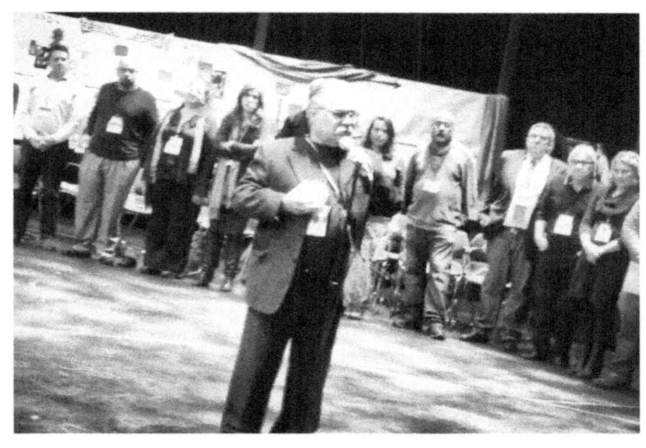

The Opening Ceremony

In the next moments, everyone assembled arranged themselves according to region into a circle snaking around the perimeter of the room. Participants who arrived to Boston from the North and Midwest; those coming from the East and West; those arriving from the South; from Miami; and finally from Texas and the Southwestern regions. As the group assembled itself, it grew larger and larger, pressing toward the limits of the space.

Kinan Valdez introduced his father, Luis Valdez, the acclaimed playwright, director, and leader of the foundational Chicano *teatro*, El Teatro Campesino. As he stepped to the center, Luis Valdez directed the formation of a circle that edged all four walls of the room:

I want you to visualize a circle, and within the circle, circumscribed by the circle, a square. This is one of the ancient symbols of the world, one of the ancient symbols of the Americas.

This moment has been five hundred years in coming. Think about that. It's beautiful to be here in Boston. The cradle of the American Revolution. But there is a continent all around this city. The Iroquois, the Maya, the Apache, the Yaqui, the Aztec. These are peoples who were here before. The Tainos, the Caribes. America was a half-world already, [a] hemisphere of ancient civilizations before the coming of any of the Europeans.

The Mayans knew the four directions. The Mayans believed in the four roads: [in] order to become completely human, everyone had to travel the four roads. They had to travel the black road, and the white road, South America and North America. They had to travel the yellow road (the East) and the red road (the West)—the path of the sun.

*So when we invoke the four directions to initiate this conference, it is not just a hollow ritual. We are invoking the ideas that promoted civilization in the Americas. These are directions fraught with meaning for everyone. You will travel all the four roads in this conference, with all their significance. We will travel the circle in the square. The feminine and the masculine. We will travel the exchanges that happen dynamically between all of these polarities. … Ultimately this is celebrating our universality. An empty word. A word that only means that we are connected to the universe. We are part of a spiraling galaxy. We have come out of a cycle of five thousand one hundred and twenty five years, the fifth sun, into the new sun, just last year. We are part of a new sun now—*el sexto sol*—and it is up to us to redefine the universe for our humanity and those that come after us. So, in that spirit, we are going to celebrate the four directions, and I ask you then to join me.* [Raises a large conch shell] *In Mayan tradition, the shell's spiral* *architecture symbolized the force of all life, the force generating the four directions, the force spinning the planet and the galaxy. The Maya used the* concha *to sing forth the power of the four directions.*

We are going to start then with an invocation to the East, the place in which the sun rises, the color yellow, where intelligence rises out of the mind, so we will all turn to the East. I ask you to raise both your hands in homage to this direction and to the idea of human intelligence. [Sounds a long note on the conch]

Turn now back to the center. And now we will turn to the north, the beginning and the end of the cycle. And so we pay homage to el norte, *to the North.* [Blows the conch] *Turn back to the center, please. Now we turn to the west, to the color red where the sun sets, the intuitive sense, the creative sense, the sense that guides all our art works and guides our sensibilities in this conference.* [Another peal of the conch] *Turn back to the center, please. And now we turn toward the South. The South. The black road, also known as the green, the blue-green road, fertility, South America. We celebrate the South.* [Sounds the conch] *Turn back to the middle. Let us invoke all of these forces in our conference, and hope that this will lead us to greater understanding and patience. We need each other to spiral, to generate forces and power. There aren't two Americas, only one America. The North and the South are coming together. The East and the West are coming together. And we will redefine the century with new ideas, the new millennium with new creativity.* [Extended moment of silence]

In advance of the Convening, each invited participant had been asked to identify an object of personal inspiration to be placed on an altar to be configured during the opening ceremony. Valdez asked the participants to open a path to a table situated in the northwest corner of the room.

This is going to be our altar. Today is Halloween; this is the eve of St. Hallow's Day, which is all souls day. November 1 and November 2 is dia de los muertos. *And so we are going to celebrate, in the spirit of* dia de los muertos, *the rebirth of all of our ideas and all of our theater concepts and movements.*

Valdez invited each participant to come to the microphone situated at the center of the circle, to speak his or her name and point of origin, and finally to offer a brief description of the item presented to the altar.

This is my offering. [Holds up a large yellow sphere.] *I bring the power of the theater of the sphere. Which is what El Teatro Campesino has been working on for almost fifty years now, the power of the farmworker, the so-called stoop labor who bring all of their humanity into the fields, to create all the food that we all eat and consume. May the world learn to respect these workers and the power of the theater of the sphere.*

Clyde Valentín moved to the microphone at the circle's center: "My name is Clyde Valentín and I hail from Brooklyn, New York. And I have this photo of Miguel Piñero and Sandra María Estevez. It was a gift from my *compañera.*" Brown University professor Patricia Ybarra stepped to the center: "I brought a line from a play by María Irene Fornés that made me stay in the theater and not become a literature professor."

And so it continued, each participant moving to the microphone, introducing herself by name, place of origin, and presenting an offering to the altar. Some offerings, like Valdez's yellow sphere, were talismanic objects—a bottle opener, an airplane boarding pass, a glass of Cuban rum—evoking an idea, a history, or a tradition. Others, like Valentín's photograph, marked the legacy of beloved family members, treasured mentors, and valued collaborators or, like Ybarra's quotation, hailed the influence or impact of a particular artist's work. Still other offerings marked a sense of place (like the ocean rock shared by playwright Elaine Romero) or the promise of possibility (like the wood molding presented by designer Regina García, which she yet hoped to use on a future set) or the passage of time (like the t-shirt shared by arts advocate Olga Garay-English, a garment she wore when attending the last national gathering of Latina/o theater artists a quarter century earlier). "I'm so proud I was there in 1986," noted Garay-English, "And I'm so proud that I'm here tonight to share this with you all."

Elena Maria Alvarado, the Artistic Director of San José's Teatro Visión, shared a small rubber *calavera* or skeleton. "It's kind of cool," she said, squeezing the skeleton until its eyes popped out cartoonishly. *[Wave of laughter]* "And this is in honor of all the wonderful *teatristas* who have played *calaveras* over the years!" *[Knowing chuckles]* "Thank you!" Center Theatre Group's Diane Rodriguez called forth. Some offerings were answered with contemplative silence, as when L.A. County Arts Commissioner Jesus Reyes placed a small plastic cross on the altar as a material proxy for his actual offering. "What I'm putting on the altar is a little private, a little thought, and I ask you to share a thought with me. But don't say it, just think it," Reyes said, "And *that's* what's going to go on the altar."

"I'm so proud I was there in 1986 and I'm so proud that I'm here tonight to share this with you all."
—Olga Garay-English

Chicago actor Ricardo Gutierrez told the story of how the image of a spinning top was one of his most vivid memories of his early childhood in Mexico. Gutierrez unspooled a top in the center of the circle. As it continued to spin, he said he once brought a box of such tops to his child's birthday, recalling how moving and funny it was to see the children struggle with the simple action of making a top spin. "It reminds me that not only do we pass down our memories," Gutierrez observed, "But we pass down so much of our work, and the cycle keeps going. … We don't keep it within ourselves; we pass it on." Gutierrez plucked the top from the floor. "And that's what I'm giving you today."

"Not only do we pass down our memories, but we pass down so much of our work, and the cycle keeps going. …We don't keep it within ourselves; we pass it on." —Ricardo Gutierrez

With each offering, emotions moved closer to the surface. As playwright-performer Luis Alfaro later described the experience, "I don't know how long it goes on because it is so deep, this ritual. I just happened to be standing next to the altar and, as some participants placed their items—a father's hat, a first play, a picture of a mentor—the emotion in their faces was overwhelming." A simple pen. A prayer card from a coworker. A necklace with a peacock feather. Some basil. A grandmother's handkerchief. A photo of a child.

When all had made their introductions and offerings, the circle was complete, and facilitator Olga Sanchez thanked the group "for sharing your stories of inspiration, for inspiring us, and for creating this altar." Sanchez reminded all assembled that the altar was "not a museum by any means. We welcome you to touch it, to pick up the stuff, to look at it, to read it, just don't take it with you. It will be up for the next three days for us to fuel ourselves, nourish ourselves, and come back to this circle." Sanchez then opened the circle for a brief break.

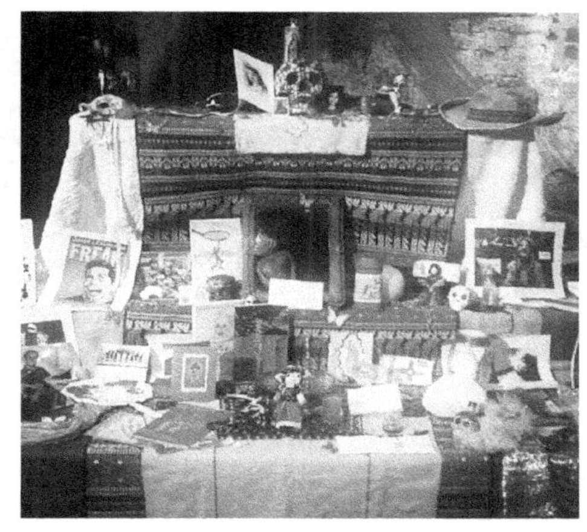

FIG. 3

The altar then stood in the space it would remain for the duration of the gathering. Photos depicting the legendary faces of United States Latina/o theater—Lupe Ontiveros, Sandra Maria Estevez, María Irene Fornés, Miguel Piñero, Hugo Medrano—stood among the piles of mementos and archival materials. Books by José Rivera, Tennessee Williams, Michelle Serros, Aristotle, Sandra Cisneros, Jean Genet, August Wilson, and María Irene Fornés were surrounded by objects with complex connections to lives and works of Latina/o theatermakers: rosaries and prayer cards, commedia masks and *calavera* heads, bottles of tequila, vodka, and rum. Interspersed among these were a mix of archival treasures: a promotional button from the Broadway run of *Zoot Suit*, original flyers and production programs from legendary *teatros*, production photos and props, a flashdrive containing everything one scholar had written on Latina/o theater. Alongside these were objects of less clear theatrical provenance: a hat, a shirt or two, a pile of uncooked rice, a crystal sphere, a *Frijolito* onesie, a handcrafted fan, assorted vintage and contemporary photographs. Crowded with this accumulation of treasures, the altar became an immediate, if impermanent, reminder of roots and of ritual, an installation marking the Convening as not only a conference, but also as a community gathering.

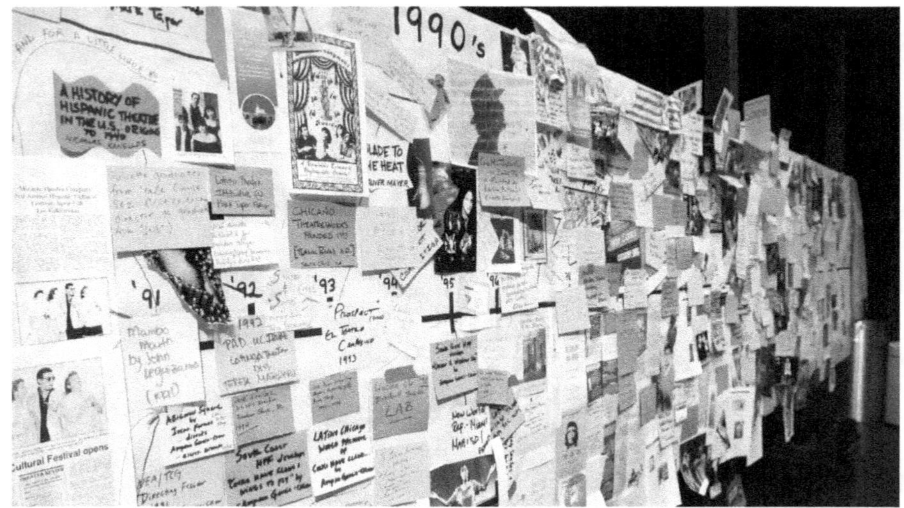

Circles Within Circles

The altar-building circle would not be the last such circle of the evening. After a brief break, the co-facilitators reconvened those assembled to undertake three more group exercises.

First, the facilitators invited the group to arrange itself again in one large circle but, rather than self-sorting according to region, the participants were asked to arrange themselves according to their number of years in the field. A dozen or so participants counted themselves as investing more than thirty-five years in the field; about thirty claimed more than two decades; twenty or so claimed a decade; and about ten claimed less than ten years in theater. The two end points of this chronology converged to create this new circle, with Luis Valdez (fifty-two years in the field) beginning a countdown that wrapped around the circle until reaching Colectivo El Pozo's Nancy García Loza, ArtsEmerson's Kevin Becerra and Teatro Luna's Abigail Vega (two years each).

Next, the participants were asked to re-sort themselves, this time into smaller groups (or "clumps") according to professional

Huerta suggested that the timeline would be "our *rebozo*, made of many colors, many textures, many ideas" marking the many "intertwining threads" of United States Latina/o theater history.

identification. Facilitator Kinan Valdez acknowledged "that everyone wears multiple hats" but encouraged each participant to self-select into one of six groupings according to his or her original creative and guiding impulse. "Meet yourselves," prompted facilitator Olga Sanchez, "and count your numbers." After a few minutes, in which members of each small group introduced themselves to each other, the facilitators called for another count off. The playwrights counted themselves to be twenty-four, the directors, twenty-one. Next came seven actors, ten scholars, eleven producers and administrators, and three designers.

Finally, the facilitators asked that everyone assist in reassembling the room into a broad semi-circle, facing the east wall, where a long panel of butcher paper hung. During the transition, Steering Committee members and HowlRound volunteers arrayed three sets of long-tables, replete with art supplies. Director Juliette Carrillo and scholar Jorge Huerta introduced the final exercise of the evening, the timeline. Huerta invited Convening participants to create "a visualization of where we have come since 1960" that might document the "evolution of United States Latina/o theater." He invited everyone to "provide information that is valuable to you, but also on behalf of people who are not here." Carrillo described the time-line as a document of both personal and professional highlights as well as field defining, watershed moments. Using different colors of paper and markers to draw connections between disparate events, Huerta suggested that the timeline would be "our *rebozo*, made of many colors, many textures, many ideas" marking the many "intertwining threads" of U.S. Latina/o theater history. "We're painting a visual landscape that expresses this journey," explained Carrillo as she encouraged all participants to join in the "controlled chaos of collective art-making." With that, Huerta and Carrillo stepped aside as participants rushed the tables to begin crafting the collective timeline, which absorbed the next twenty-five minutes but would continue throughout the weekend.

At the end of the three-hour opening session, co-facilitator Clyde Valentín invited the group to reflect on "this very brief day" and to "shout out one word…that comes to you when you think about how you feel in this moment." Those assembled offered their summation of the day:

> *Humble!*
> *Hungry!*
> *More!*
> *Electric!*
> *Inspired!*
> *Old!*
> *Surreal!*
> *Honored!*
> *Storytellers!*
> Orgullo*!*
> *Blessed!*

With that, the group dispersed for the evening.

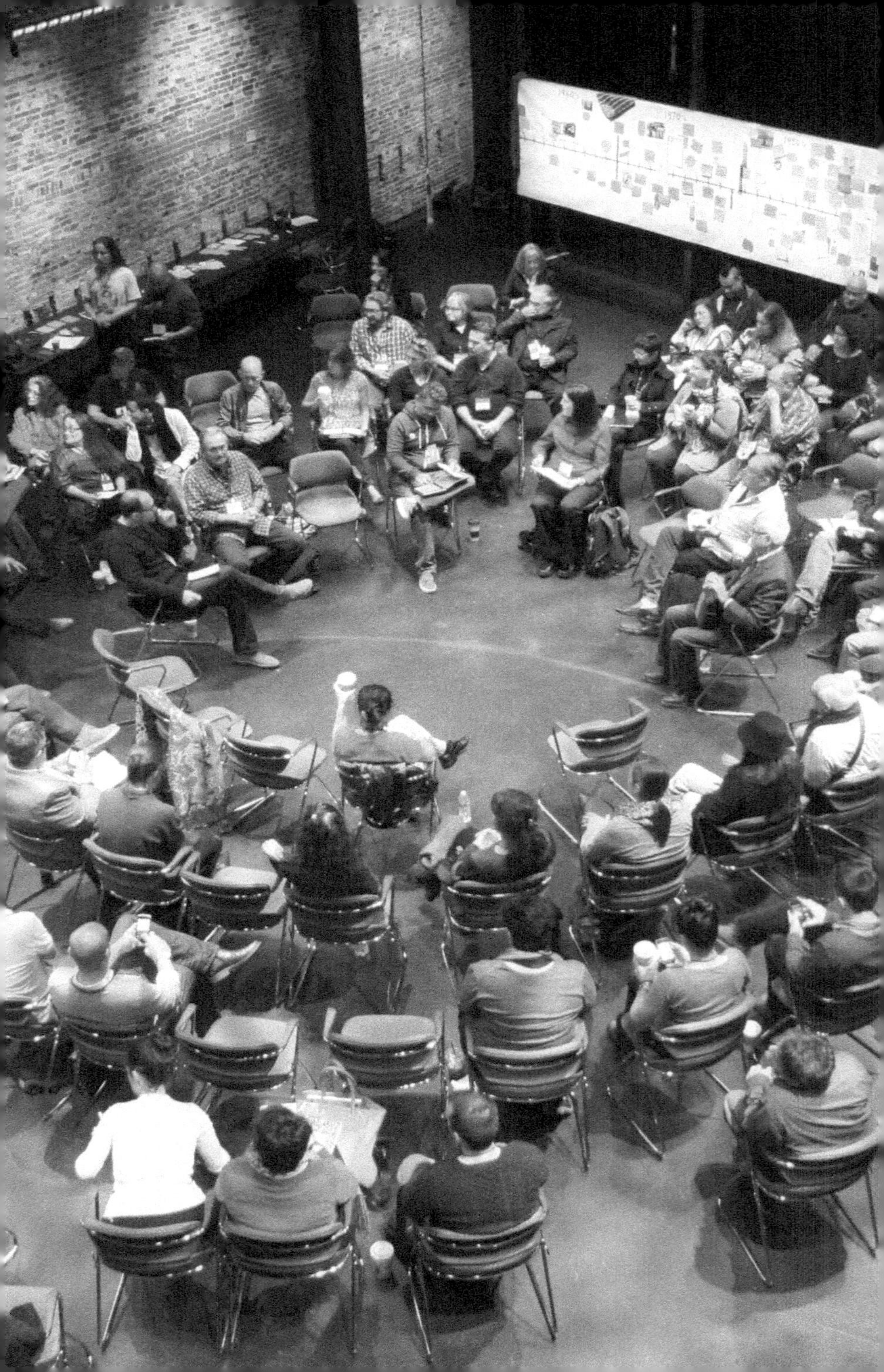

Friday 1 November

"We exist. We are here. We are entitled to poetry." —Migdalia Cruz

The Convening's second day began and concluded with *conocimiento* groups or small-group conversations. This *conocimiento* model—breaking Convening participants into seven or eight roughly equal-sized groups according to shared knowledge, experience or perspective—recurred throughout the gathering. Friday's structure was guided by the meeting of, and presentation by, seven affinity groups according to engagement with profession.

The groups gathered those working primarily: 1) in regional theaters; 2) in community-based and/or culturally-specific groups; 3) in academia; 4) and 5) as independent artists; 6) in international groups; or 7) in ensembles. *Conocimiento* groups met first thing, and then again after the three Listening Circles. These conversations thereby provided a guiding thread through the entire second day of Convening activities, which culminated with brief performance/presentations by each *conocimiento* group at day's end.

Each of the Listening Circles was dedicated to open conversations from practitioners occupying different roles in the process of making Latina/o theater. The first Listening Circle heard from "The Creators," those directly involved in composing, developing, or devising work. The second listened to "The Translators," those collaborators—actors, directors, designers, adaptors—charged with bringing works to the stage. The third attended to the voices of "The Pillars," those administrators, producers, and academics charged with bringing work to various publics. At the outset of each Listening Circle, the session's designated moderator welcomed the ten or so invited contributors to sit in the inner circle to begin their conversation, typically around questions pre-circulated among the invitees. At different moments (sometimes at roughly the halfway mark, sometimes at other junctures), the moderator opened the circle so that the conversation might include additional voices for the remainder of the allotted time.

To insure that each Listening Circle's smaller conversation would open to a larger one, the Convening's organizers melded "long table" and "fishbowl" approaches to staging a dynamic public conversation. Thus, in preparation for the Listening Session, the configuration of Emerson's Liebergott Black Box was arranged in the "fish bowl" style, with ten to twelve chairs arranged facing inward at the center of the space, and with the remaining chairs arrayed in larger concentric circles around the inner circle. Each Listening Circle's moderator guided the conversation according to the "long-table" format devised by artist Lois Weaver.

The "long table" adopts and adapts the metaphor of a dinner party ("where conversation is the only course") as an alternate, open-ended, non-hierarchical model for staging public inquiry. To provide a general introduction to the "long table" premise, Convening organizers scattered printouts of Weaver's "etiquette sheet" on seats throughout the space. In preparation for the first Listening Circle, the facilitators

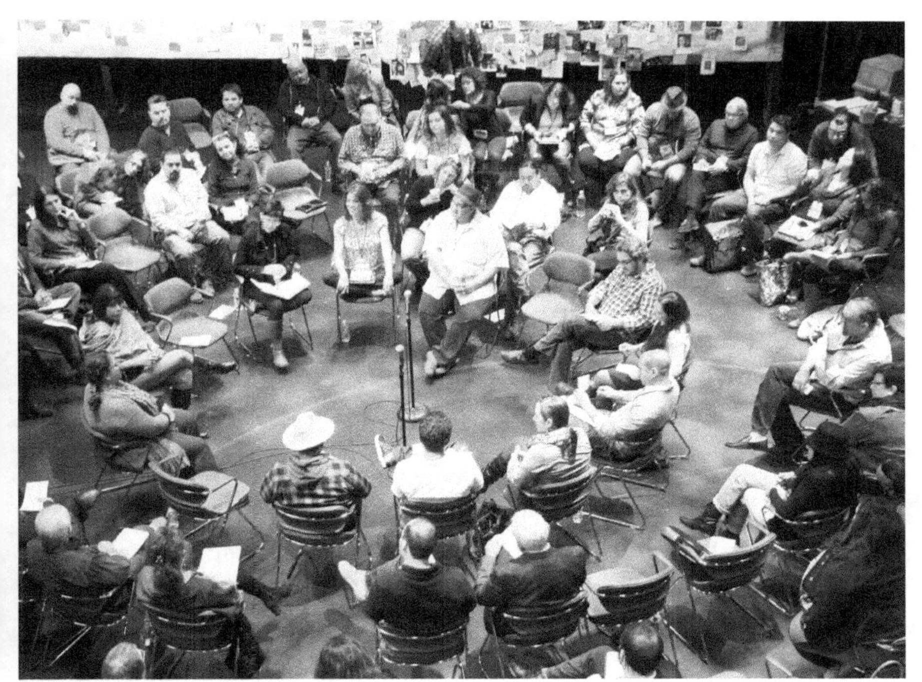

guided the group in a spontaneous, choral reading of the principles of long-table conversation (including such prompts as "There can be silence," "Awkward pauses are to be expected," and "Laughter is welcome"). Facilitators and moderators reminded everyone that each Listening Circle would begin as a conversation at first "closed" but later "opened" so that anyone might join the inner circle (as per long table etiquette) simply by claiming a seat or by requesting that a seat be opened.

For more on the Long Table concept, go to publicaddresssystems.org. For "fish bowl" strategies, search kstoolkit.org.

Listening Sessions

LISTENING SESSION 1: **The Creators**

Diane Rodriguez, Associate Producer at Los Angeles's Center Theatre Group and current President of the Board of Directors of Theatre Communications Group (TCG), moderated the first Listening Circle. Joining Rodriguez in the inner circle were: Chicago-based actor/playwright Christopher De Paola; Juan Amador (DJ Wonway) of San Francisco's Campo Santo; playwright/performer Richard Montoya of the Los Angeles-based ensemble Culture Clash; playwright Migdalia Cruz; playwright/producer Georgina H. Escobar; dramaturg Lydia Garcia of Oregon Shakespeare Festival; playwright Luis Alfaro; playwright Octavio Solis; and actor/producer Abigail Vega of Chicago's Teatro Luna. At the outset, Rodriguez explained to the larger circle that, in preparation for the session, she had posed some particular questions to the inner circle via email. She asked the inner circle whether there were questions that made an impact and that the artists wanted to address first.

Actor-playwright Christopher De Paola answered: "The question that spoke to me the most was, 'Do you think that you deserve special treatment because you are Latina/o?'" *[Laughter from the inner group punctuated by murmurs of "yes!" from the outer circle]* De Paola asserted, "Absolutely not…but the institution has now trained me to feel like I deserve some." Rodriguez pressed De Paola to elaborate. He explained, "the institution of the theater told me I was a Latino artist" and even after almost twenty years into his career, he sometimes felt "really lost in the landscape" between being an entertainer and being a Latino-identified artist. After some rumination, he asked, "I feel very blessed to be in this group [but] I'm just struggling…do I belong in all this?" Octavio Solis asked De Paola to clarify "what do you mean—belong in all this?" To Solis' query, De Paola added a few rhetorical questions about the question of identity in the arts, including "What is a Latino artist? What is a Latino play? Where do I land in all this?"

De Paola's queries instigated an array of responses. Others weighed in on how their experience of Latina/o identity informed their experience of "belonging" in the theater. Some expressed affinity for De Paola's uncertainty, while others affirmed their answer to De Paola's question. Playwright Migdalia Cruz did so emphatically:

> *You are at the table. When I first started, there were a lot of tables that didn't want me there. You invite yourself. This is who I am. I want to be here. Feed me. Or I am going to be over your shoulder, taking stuff off your plate. Who you identify as, is who you are. And you should always feel welcome at any table. …I'm empowered by my identity, and I carry it with me wherever I go. …It's such a fabulous blessing, and it actually gives us something to create art about.*

Playwright Octavio Solis engaged the question of "special treatment" somewhat differently. "I expect to be treated differently for being a playwright in the room," Solis began. "If I'm not being treated specially for what I bring as an artist to the table, then I really wonder why I'm there—then I really wonder if they brought me in because I am a Latino."

For others, the tension between being a Latina/o artist and a sense of artistic belonging stirred additional questions. Culture

Clash's Richard Montoya asked where Latina/o creative community might be found amidst the competitive scramble of contemporary theater. Montoya wondered whether competition pitted Latina/o artists against one another, whether it "allow[ed] institutions to exoticize: 'Well, who's the best? Who's the youngest? Who is more East Coast? And who is more West Coast?'" Diane Rodriguez pressed the question of competition, asking if it manifested in Latina/o artists against other Latina/o artists for opportunities and resources or whether comparison to other Latina/o artists also raised the bar for one's work. "Coming from the hip-hop aesthetic," replied Juan Amador (DJ Wonway),

> *We use competitiveness to push each other and to evolve farther. I just sit in a circle like this and I feel like I'm just the weakest link here. I can't do this… But simply because I know, if I'm the weakest link, I'm gonna step the hell up and I'm gonna at least try to keep up, if not make you doubt yourself.* [Rumble of laughter] *But not in a bad way! But just to be, like, shit! Let's take it to another level. …It raises my game.*

Chantal Rodriguez, Programming Director and Literary Manager of Los Angeles's Latino Theater Company, agreed. "We just had an L.A. theater *encuentro*, where we saw just how much Latina/o theater is happening every weekend in Los Angeles, and people have asked [about competition] as well." She continued, "[it] shouldn't be competitive. Just because they go to your show, doesn't mean they won't come to my show. The more people that are going to Latina/o theater, the better. … It really creates a stronger network and community." But the abundance of distinctive and worthy Latina/o work brought additional challenges, noted Lydia Garcia, Literary Associate at Oregon Shakespeare Festival. "What makes it so hard for me as a dramaturg and as a Latina in an institution [where I am] part of conversations about season selection,"

Garcia observed, is that "as artists of color we are [often] competing with each other, for that one or that second slot, and invariably in the smaller spaces." Garcia reflected how "my identity as a Latina and as an artist who's at an institution" becomes "wrapped up with this sense of competition" and the question, "how do I weigh this every day." Diane Rodriguez pressed the group to "excavate that reality we live in" and share "our strategies to get more of our arts produced in the multilayered theatrical ecosystem that we live in."

Playwright Octavio Solis offered a strategy premised upon an ethic of mutual advocacy. "If we know a play that we can't do, we should recommend it aggressively," Solis asserted. "Do this play," Rodriguez interjected. "Yes, do this play," Solis continued. "Get the word out about that work." Playwright and performer Luis Alfaro offered a somewhat different riff on the shape mutual advocacy might take. "We have to do a very generous subversion of every institution that we go to," he observed, describing his own experiences working closely with marketing and box office personnel at different theaters. Framing this work within the "concept of service" that he was raised with, Alfaro asserted that artists should also advocate for diversity within a theater's audiences, boards, and company staff. Affirming that the primary strategy must be "to write the best fucking plays we

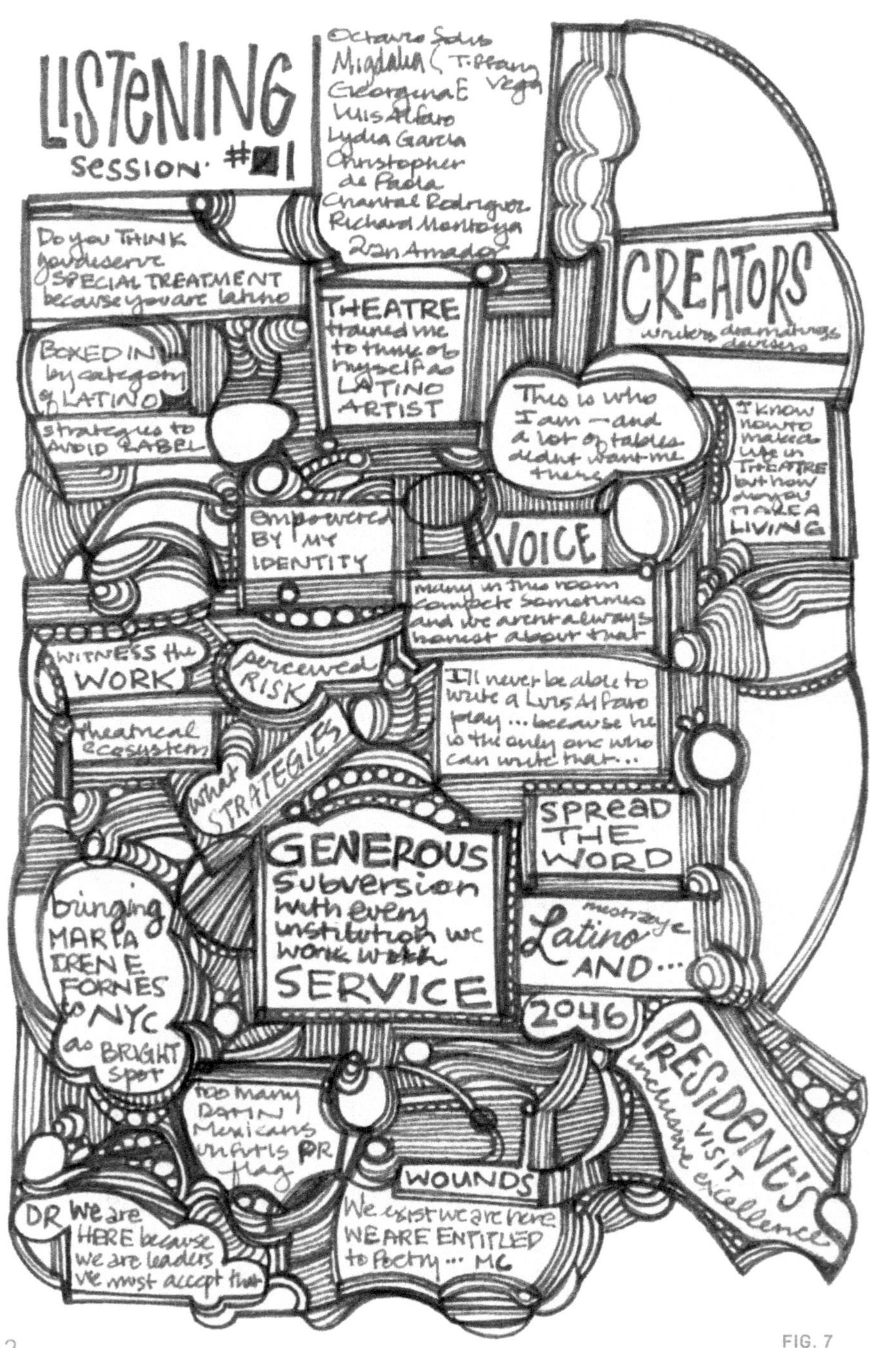

LISTENING SESSION #1
Octavio Solis
Migdalia (T.Pearro)
Georgina E Vega
Luis Alfaro
Lydia Garcia
Christopher de Paola
Chantal Rodriguez
Richard Montoya
Zan Amador
CREATORS
writers dramaturgs devisers
Do you THINK you deserve SPECIAL TREATMENT because you are latino
BOXED IN by category of LATINO
strategies to AVOID LABEL
THEATRE trained me to think of myself as LATINO ARTIST
This is who I am — and a lot of tables didn't want me there
I know how to make a life in THEATRE but how do you MAKE A LIVING
empowered BY MY IDENTITY
VOICE
Many in this room conflict sometimes and we aren't always honest about that
WITNESS the WORK
perceived RISK
theatrical ecosystem
what STRATEGIES
I'll never be able to write a Luis Alfaro play ... because he is the only one who can write that ...
SPREAD THE WORD
GENEROUS subversion with every institution we work with SERVICE
most saye Latino AND ...
bringing MARIA IRENE FORNES to NYC as BRIGHT spot
2046
PRESIDENTS visit inclusive excellence
too many DAMN Mexicans un artis PR flag
WOUNDS
DR We are HERE because we are leaders we must accept that
We exist we are here WE ARE ENTITLED to Poetry ... MC

FIG. 7

can write," but right behind that must come strategies to advocate for diverse work within a particular institution and to connect to the communities most served by his plays. For Alfaro, the question of "How am I going to work toward my own authenticity" was necessarily and immediately followed by a second question, "How do I bring [my authenticity] into the community?" Teatro Luna's Abigail Vega echoed the importance of being attentive and responsive to the diversity of *Latinidad*, especially in terms of race, gender, and age, so that audiences never are the ones to wonder, "Do I belong here?" when attending a Latina/o play.

Returning to the theme of the abundance of Latina/o theater work being done, Richard Montoya noted, "Witnessing each other's work is a generous act." Playwright and producer Georgina H. Escobar noted the importance of supporting young artists to "just do the work" by whatever means necessary (crowdsourcing, touring, pop up theaters). On this point, Vega argued that going to see the work of emerging Latina/o artists who are putting their work out there, whether in your town or touring through, was itself an essential form of advocacy.

Referencing the recent success of Teatro Luna's tour, both in artistic terms and in terms of community-building, Diane Rodriguez noted, "Teatro Luna's tour was one of the real bright spots this year," and then asked those assembled in the inner circle to add their own "bright spots."

Migdalia Cruz responded first with a moving testimonial about the impact of the national theater community's support of the efforts to move influential playwright María Irene Fornés to a long-term care facility nearer Fornés' communities in New York City. "The fact that the theater community, especially on the East Coast, rallied around her…meant so much," Cruz explained. "It also made me feel, well, very hopeful about the theater community because, most of the time, I hate y'all." *[Huge laugh]* "Damn," Cruz continued, "We do love each other, even if we don't always take the time to say it." Cruz rummaged in her bag. "I was so suspicious of this conference, like there's too many damn Mexicans, what's gonna happen?" Cruz stood and unfurled the flag of Puerto Rico. [*Room erupts with cheers, applause, and laughter*] "So! Puerto Rico is in the house! And you may not like me, but I'm still your sister."

Chantal Rodriguez added to the list of bright spots, reporting on one of the initiatives emerging from the Los Angeles *encuentro*. A committee dedicated to seeing new Latina/o works throughout the greater Los Angeles area had been formed, with plans to develop a report on all the work being created. "Let's see each other's work…and let's talk about it."

"Not surprisingly," quipped Richard Montoya, "I was my own bright spot this year." Montoya reflected on the moment he realized that, as both a playwright and as a member of an ensemble, he had a hand in three major productions at regional theaters in California, all running the same weekend—productions that had provided thirty Equity contracts to thirty California actors.

At this juncture, the circle opened—somewhat abruptly—to welcome the President of Emerson College, Lee Pelton, who stood at the circle's center to welcome the Convening participants and affirm his belief in "diversity at the center of excellence." Following President Pelton's brief remarks, Rodriguez opened the circle formally, inviting others to join the conversation with their own questions or observations.

Playwright and Artistic Director of Los Angeles' Casa 0101, Josefina López took a seat in the circle and queried the group: "What sort of wounds are you writing about?" In a quick round robin, the inner circle engaged the question from a variety of perspectives. Luis Alfaro reflected upon how his good fortune of having five world premieres in a year reminded him of the urgency and power of "giving voice to silenced experience." Christopher De Paola shared his passion for addressing the "societal wound" that removes theater from the experience of many middle and working-class people. Juan Amador shared that "My father was killed in the Nicaraguan revolution before I was born" and noted how his work was bringing him closer to connecting with his Nicaraguan family roots. Migdalia Cruz answered, "My wound is my original wound." Cruz then briefly shared the story of her

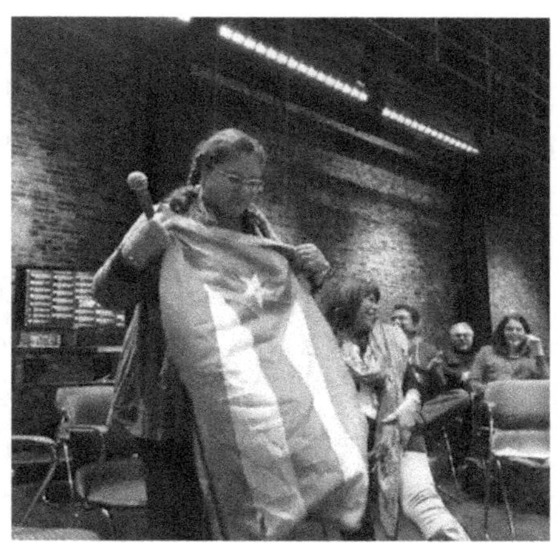

childhood best friend's brutal rape and murder. "I feel that everything I write," Cruz explained, "is about giving voice to the disenfranchised. We exist. We are here. We are entitled to poetry."

Next to enter the circle was Mario Ernesto Sánchez, founder and Producing Artistic Director of Miami's International Hispanic Theatre Festival. Sánchez asked whether the Latina/o theater community would be "ready"—artistically or organizationally—for 2046, the year in which Latinas/os are expected to comprise the majority of United States residents. Georgina H. Escobar's answer emphasized her hope that Latina/o artists as "spiritual creatives" might be "consciousness beacons" for increased awareness about environmental crises facing the planet, while Josefina López affirmed her hope that attention to population growth would not come "at the cost of women giving up their dreams." Alfaro asserted the importance of "consciousness raising" about the often-untapped Latina/o creative talents, especially among designers and directors, as part of creative preparedness, and Chantal Rodriguez emphasized the urgency of breaking down the paradigms of privilege that situated Latinas/os ever and always as "other."

Playwright Maria Alexandria Beech then took a seat in the circle. With measured but palpable emotion, Beech asserted that activism—especially "calling out how we're shut out" and "how works are offensive"—needed "to be contextualized as difficult work." Beech went on to insist that Latina/o artists needed to "stop kissing people's asses, because we're not there yet" and to be "courageous enough to be hated for speaking the truth." Director José Carrasquillo then stepped both into the circle and into the space opened by Beech's emphatic intervention. His words evoked those uttered by Migdalia Cruz almost an hour earlier. "We can create our own table. We are powerful. We know our stories. We know where we come from, where we are going. And, yes, we will be ready for 2046, because we are here today!" Dramaturg and scholar Tiffany Ana López then joined the circle to ask, "How can we create spaces where creative pain can be honored?"

Next, playwright Tanya Saracho joined the circle to comment on the impact of economic instability upon Latina/o artists. Drawing upon her experiences navigating both "building your own space" and "being in the larger spaces," Saracho asserted that economic security remained elusive, which caused her to question the sustainability of an artistic career. "I know how we make a life in the theater," Saracho observed, "But how do we make a living?"

Olga Garay-English, then the Executive

Director of Los Angeles's Department of Cultural Affairs, stepped into
the circle and extended Saracho's query about economic precariousness.
"Yes, there are a lot of powerful people here from the artistic side, but
we are not powerful from the economic side. We may be the majority," Garay-English continued, "but we are not an economic majority."
Garay-English proposed that Latina/o theatermakers begin to demand
that every funder be "brought to task" on whether they are serving the
Latina/o community effectively and equitably. "We better get smart,"
admonished Garay-English, "Or 2046 is going to come and we're going
to be as under-resourced as we are now."

"We better get smart. Or 2046 is going to come and we're going to
be as under-resourced as we are now." —Olga Garay-English

Picking up the threads of preparedness, advocacy, and sustainability
introduced by Sánchez, Beech, Saracho, and Garay-English, moderator
Diane Rodriguez invited the full circle to share "models of surviving."

Luis Alfaro observed that "being a teacher" is both "a way of making money and also a way of being a better artist." While several others
agreed that academia provided particular opportunities for Latina/o
artists to, in the words of Chantal Rodriguez "infiltrate and to represent," others affirmed the importance of patronage support, both for
individual artists and for institutions. "Life is getting finite and narrow,"
Richard Montoya interjected, reminding the group of a story widely
attributed to Mexican-American actor Anthony Quinn, "An actor in Europe is always an artist, whether you're working or not. An out-of-work
actor in the States is a bum." Montoya posed the question, "Why don't
we have access to the controlled monopolies that are arts non-profits?"

This discussion about survival again stirred the questions of identity—individual and institutional—that had simmered throughout the conversation, and these concerns guided the session toward its conclusion. Rose Cano, of Seattle's eSe Teatro, wondered about "making our own labels and tables." Diane Rodriguez replied emphatically, "This Convening comes from a sense of power. We are here because we are leaders. Let's just accept that. We've moved very far. We are creating our own table." Playwright and director Cándido Tirado observed that "part of what bigger theaters want is the Latina/o audience," as he reflected on the ways that larger theaters sometimes held the Latina/o artist responsible for failing to attract a Latina/o audience even as those theaters often failed to offer a reciprocal commitment to either the Latina/o artist or the Latina/o audience. Tirado asked, "What do we bring?" Rodriguez replied, "That's your power. The people that you bring."

"We're right on this place of a precipice, really" asserted Christopher Acebo, the Associate Artistic Director of Oregon Shakespeare Festival, "The secret of 2046 is not lost on the institutions of this country." Acebo raised questions and concerns about the adaptability of larger theater institutions. "How do we even assume that inviting an audience is going to be the way that that audience is going to come? We have not built that trust over decades and decades. How can we work within those institutions to anchor them with Latina/o audiences?" Playwright Octavio Solis and David Lozano, Executive Artistic Director of Dallas's Cara Mía Theatre, then spoke up to complicate the picture. Solis pointedly asked about how the larger theater's "interest" in the Latina/o audience would "impact the smaller *teatros* who have been dedicated to the Latina/o audience." Lozano expressed concern about the demands placed on smaller, culturally-specific organizations—that they be a "policeman" of the cultural content presented by larger organizations without reciprocal support to fortify their own organizational and artistic development. Lozano asked whether HowlRound might help to mediate such encounters between organizations of different scale. "We need some sort guidance," Lozano asserted. "We need this contact with national networks."

"That's what is being built here," Rodriguez concluded. "Conversation amongst each other is so important, so that we know how we feed into each other and support each other." As Rodriguez brought the Listening Session to its close, the co-facilitators encouraged participants to continue to work over lunch by self-selecting into mutual mentorship groups and asking questions of "those who might mentor you."

LISTENING SESSION 2: The Translators

After the "mutual mentorship" lunch, the group reconvened for the second Listening Session, moderated by Karen Zacarías, former playwright-in-residence at Washington D.C.'s Arena Stage. Zacarías was joined in the inner circle by a group of about a dozen directors, actors, designers, and other artists, including: freelance directors José Carrasquillo, Juliette Carrillo, Daniel Jáquez, Jerry Ruiz, and Laurie Woolery; vocal coach Micha Espinosa of Arizona State University; Chicago-based actor Sandra Delgado; Christopher Acebo, designer and Associate Artistic Director of Oregon Shakespeare Festival; playwright and scholar Irma Mayorga of Dartmouth College; designer Regina García; and interdisciplinary director/performer Marc David Pinate. Zacarías encouraged the participants to use the session to "say bold, brave things. …If we're not going to say them here, where are we going to say them?"

Zacarías invited both the inner and outer circles to call forth their answers to the following question: What is the one thing you never want to hear again in the American theater?

Actor Sandra Delgado was the first to speak: "I never want to hear another critic compare a Latina/o play to a telenovela." *[Cheers]* Zacarías pressed Delgado to offer a solution. "I don't know how to resolve that,"

Delgado affirmed. "I had no idea that middle-aged white critics were so well-versed in the genre of the telenovela. [We need] Latina/o critics!"

Director Laurie Woolery offered another answer to Rodriguez's question: "There's not enough Latina/o talent out there." Zacarías asked Woolery to suggest a strategy for confronting that claim, and Woolery suggested two: "Producing our own work [and] encouraging them to look deeper."

Answers to questions posed by Zacarías, first from the inner circle and then from the circle as a whole, echoed themes first raised by Delgado and Woolery, especially regarding the limited cultural literacy of theatrical decision-makers and the unreasonable burdens placed on Latina/o theatermakers to resolve systemic problems.

"Obviously, we have some obstacles," Zacarías noted before asking a next question: "What was some of the best advice anyone ever gave you?" The conversation then turned toward principles of guidance as participants, in both the inner and outer circles, offered their reflections on clarifying moments along their professional paths. The names of many mentors and inspirations—Oskar Eustis, María Irene Fornés, Raúl Julia, Mark Lamos, and many in attendance in the room—were heard. In summary, particular themes recurred, with most acts of guidance taking the form of granting permission or providing witness.

After sharing stories of inspiration and guidance, Zacarías posed another question. Noting that one of the recurrent themes expressed in the surveys circulated prior to the convening was the desire on the part of Latina/o artists not only to be trusted to take on Latina/o work, but also to have the opportunity to do work that was not Latina/o. So, Zacarías asked, "Why? Why do we want to do work that doesn't talk

"What is the one thing you never want to hear again?"

On the limited Latina/o cultural competence of theatrical gate-keepers:

- There's not enough Latino talent out there.
- There are Latina/os in the South?
- A reviewer's description of the community producing a community-based work as impoverished, with no indication of any prior knowledge of, or inquiry into, the community's complexity.
- Another reviewer's praise for "fiery, hot, chili-pepper timing."
- That actor just doesn't look Latina/o.
- That's not a Latina/o play.

On the expectations placed upon Latina/o theatermakers:

- You look so American.
- Could you add some Spanish? Could you spice it up?
  Could you be more urban? Can you do that with an accent?
- There's just not a big enough audience for a Mexican-American play.
- English-speaking audiences will feel left out.
- It's great but could you add more men to this?
- You can be gay, or you can be Latino, but not both in the same play.
- You know what you should do…

On the assumptions impeding Latina/o theatermakers equitable access to opportunity:

- We're not doing a Latina/o play this year.
- I know s/he is not Latina/o but s/he is really good. S/he can play Latina/o.
- Latina/o actors don't have the training. They're just not ready.
- Why do you have to have a Latina lead when there aren't Latina actresses of that age?
- There aren't Latina/o directors who can direct a LORT play.
- But we already gave to [major LORT theater] to do their Latina/o play.
- I saw that there was a Latino play in the season, and I was really concerned…
- If you are good enough, we'll hear about you.

about the Latina/o experience?"

"We are storytellers," explained director Juliette Carrillo, "We want to live and breathe and taste and feel and smell all kinds of worlds. It's a great opportunity to live in an Arthur Miller world or a Lorraine Hansberry world—to be inside of that reality." Designer Chris Acebo added, "Wearing my designer's hat very clearly, I think of myself as a visual interpreter of a writer's words and, as an interpreter, you want to interpret everything." Director Lisa Portes joined the circle to say, "I didn't set out to do plays by women of color, but those are the plays I'm attracted to. I just think, you know, as an artist you have to go wherever your heart goes." Actor and teacher Sandra Marquez expanded the conversation beyond questions of artistic vision toward the discrepancies between how an artist is trained and how an artist is (and is not) able to work. "I'm a craftsman," Marquez explained, "I'm very invested in my culture, *pero*, before that I'm a human being, so let me tell the fucking human being stories." Later, scholar and playwright Irma Mayorga expressed the question of reciprocity embedded in one's artistic desire to do Latina/o work and also be considered for work outside the Latina/o experience. "Sure, I want to try out different aesthetics [but] I'm also a person who is bicultural," Mayorga explained, "Translation has been my whole life—bilingual, bicultural—[so] of course I know Shakespeare. …Have you met my Latina/o playwrights?" Mayorga concluded, "That's where I start to become very discomfited by someone touring in my cultural world."

Earlier in the conversation, director and translator Daniel Jáquez had raised concerns about the degree to which an individual Latina/o artist should be responsible or accountable to other Latina/o artists, especially with regard to providing access to opportunity. "We want access," asserted Jáquez, "I'm more upset with Latino playwrights who don't give opportunities to Latino directors and Latino actors because they want to move [to] the next step. …I don't get upset if a non-Latino is working on a Latino play, but there has to be a reason." Playwright Tanya Saracho was the first to engage Jáquez's question directly, "It's very hard to pitch the Latino director. There's an approved list." Saracho went on to describe the "challenge" of pitching her first-choice Latina/o directors to artistic directors, only to be rebuffed with statements like

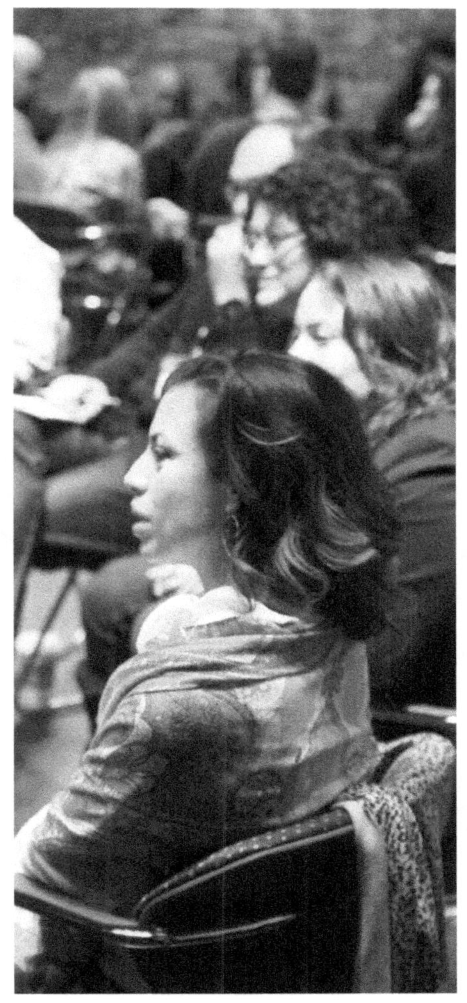

FIG. 9

"maybe in a few years," or "we just want the best person for the job." Expressing her frustration, Saracho continued, "So you don't know what those playwright's have been through. …I'm never going to stop pitching [Latina/o directors…] but it's really difficult because there is a 'list.'" Freelance director José Carrasquillo then added, "That unfortunately is a reality that we all face. There are levels. And I continue to believe

[that] our responsibility is to also…to really educate some of the artistic directors, some of the people who make decisions." Carrasquillo concluded that "[we] must continue to fight and to educate people to be part of the conversation."

José Luis Valenzuela, Artistic Director of the Latino Theater Company at the Los Angeles Theatre Center, then joined the circle to challenge the conversation's emphasis on access to certain kinds of theaters. Reflecting on his own decision to leave United States regional theaters to work in Europe nearly two decades prior, Valenzuela said, "I think the conversation should be different [than] trying to get ourselves on a list, be part of the club." Valenzuela then offered what he called a "reality check." Valenzuela asserted, "American Theater is in a crisis, and we have to include ourselves as part of that crisis. If artistically, if you have to aim at what we see in regional theaters, we're in trouble." Echoing

Valenzuela's concern about what she called "this lusting after the regional companies," Elisa Marina Alvarado of Teatro Visión added, "I ask for an acknowledgment of the Latino companies that for many years have been fully committed to doing your work. …Put in your eyesight the companies that have been there for you and will continue to be there for you." Responding to both Valenzuela and Alvarado, freelance director Lisa Portes rejoined the circle to add: "There is a reality of money for every actor, for every designer, for every director, for every writer." Then, invoking Olga Garay-English's earlier assessment of Latina/o philanthropy, Portes insisted, "We have to raise more money for our theaters to fund us at the levels we need to be funded in order to survive."

The conversation quickly turned to a consideration of the complex interconnections throughout the "ecosystem" of Latina/o theatermaking, as individual Latina/o artists move between larger and smaller companies, always struggling to make both a living and a life. Playwright Enrique Urueta emphasized the importance of breaking down the theatrical hierarchy through an orientation toward mentorship of the next generation "as opposed to 'I've already gotten here—when you get here, we'll talk.'" Richard Montoya affirmed the artistic value of working in both big theaters and storefronts, of "cross[ing] that street many, many times." Even as she acknowledged the financial difficulties of making a living as a director in regional theater, Juliette Carrillo also reminded the group that working in the regionals was not simply careerist but also about "visibility, infiltrating the mainstream" because "in the end we want to be seen and heard." Vocal coach and educator Micha Espinosa also underscored the importance of visibility for her students who "see how Latina/o theater is marginalized in the academy, how it's marginalized financially, professionally" which can lead younger Latina/o artists to deemphasize "their roots" as artists because there are so few evident rewards for becoming self-identified Latina/o theater artists. Designer and educator Regina García agreed, "Earlier when we were saying 'American Theater is in crisis'—the way we teach American Theater is also in crisis."

As a gesture toward conclusion, moderator Karen Zacarías invited the group to reflect on their "dream project." Reminding the group that "the interest of the Latina/o Theatre Commons is to make the future brighter," Zacarías invited those assembled to consider "saying it out loud…maybe something magical will happen."

Designer Regina García reflected on her hunger for a creative,

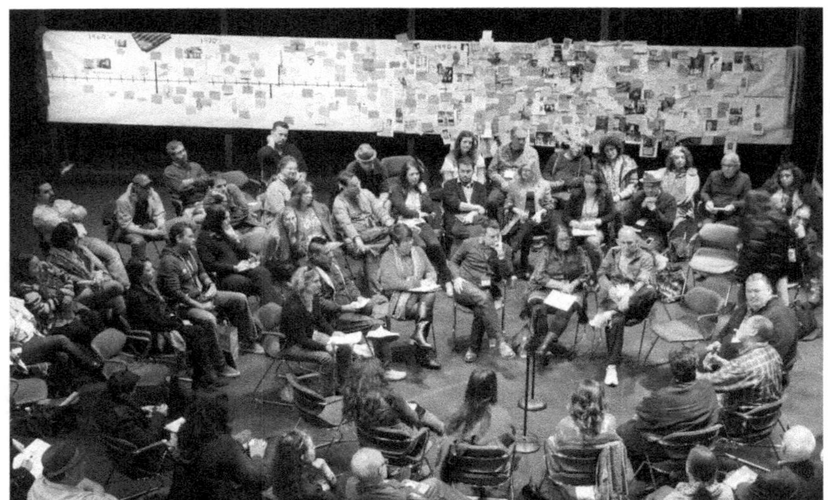

collaborative laboratory for the development of new Latina/o plays. Director Daniel Jáquez shared the vision of INTAR's new initiatives to "support the young generation" of emerging Latina/o actors and directors, especially those not coming out of the established training programs. Marc David Pinate shared his vision for a "theater ashram" where the space exists for practitioners "to offer classes in the arts of conjuring" and then develop community-based festivals to exchange and "share their skills and expertise."

Chris Acebo then asked the room to note the "expansiveness of this conversation." Acebo reflected on the many voices and aspirations expressed in the previous hour—from working abroad to working locally, working in the regional theaters and working in the streets—as he observed, emphatically, "All of it has great value, and we are an amazing, diverse group of people that can have all of that."

"I have the privilege of being one of the oldest participants here," Luis Valdez noted, "so I have the advantage of perspective." Valdez reflected on his own and El Teatro Campesino's experiences performing first for community-based audiences, then for more "mainstream"

American audiences, and most recently for an international Latin American audience. Valdez told the story of El Teatro Campesino's first New York performance in 1967 before an audience made up of two thousand activists, including five hundred striking workers. He contrasted that "wonderful experience" with the one a decade or so later when *Zoot Suit* arrived on Broadway. "I think the truth about *Zoot Suit* in 1979 is that we were thirty years too soon," Valdez said. "But we broke the ice. With our heads! But we broke the ice." Then, after a brief aside about the utility of the term "Latino" ("much too general to be of use to anybody…an adjective that we're using as a noun"), Valdez reflected on the "astounding experience" of staging the world premiere of the Spanish-language *Zoot Suit* at Teatro Nacional in Mexico City. Describing himself as an "*hijo de los campesinos,*" Valdez mused on the paradox of being an "*ex-pocho*" and teaching "*Mexicanos* how to be Chicano." Valdez also spoke about the resources invested in his play's production in Mexico. "They spent some bucks on this, some pesos!" Valdez recalled, "And you know what—I got paid! I got royalties and I got paid for directing. I was almost ashamed. I didn't have to cross the desert. I flew in!" The sustained success of *Zoot Suit* in Mexico and Latin America verified for Valdez the fact that "what we say about ourselves here can play across the border, can play in America Latina!" Turning his experience into counsel for the playwrights in the room, Valdez continued, "I suggest you think of your work in terms of the international scope. Get your plays translated into Spanish. They will do you there! It isn't just a question of relating to the United States. It's a question of relating to America!" *[Burst of applause]*

Chair of Americans for the Arts and Associate Producing Director of GALA Hispanic Theatre in Washington D.C., Abel López opened the session with a reminder that "even though this [session] is about administrators, this is a very creative group of people." Noting that most of those joining López in the inner circle were artists as well as administrators, López underscored the "duality and multifaceted roles that we play… we are all part of a larger ecosystem…" López addressed the Listening Session's inner circle: "We want you to speak from your perspective as leaders of organizations within your communities" as well as "part of a larger field."

Joining López in the center circle were a group of about a dozen producers, administrators, scholars, and other arts leaders. The inner circle included artistic and executive directors of companies from across the country, including Alexandra Meda of Teatro Luna; Tony Garcia of Denver's Su Teatro; Alberto Justiano, founder of Teatro del Pueblo in St. Paul; Anthony Rodriguez of Atlanta's Aurora Theatre; Elisa Marina Alvarado of Teatro Visión in San Jose, California; David Lozano of Dallas' Cara Mía Theatre Company; Ivan Vega of Chicago's Urban-Theater Company; and Josefina López, playwright and founding Artistic Director of CASA 0101 in Los Angeles. In addition, the panel included producer Jacob Padrón of Chicago's Steppenwolf Theatre; Marissa Chibas, CalArts professor and director of Duende CalArts; Patricia Ybarra, professor at Brown University and President-Elect of the Association for Theatre in Higher Education; Rose Portillo, Associate Director of Los Angeles About Productions; and Tiffany Vega, Marketing and Administrative Associate at HI-ARTS in New York.

To open conversation among these "pillars" of Latina/o theater, moderator López prompted: "We don't have to wait for demographic change. …What is the dream you have for your organization?"

Many envisioned a future of artistic growth. Cara Mía's David

Lozano dreamed of having "the most trained, and most capable, and most inspired" performers, designers, and board of directors. Ivan Vega dreamed of "creating access" and "opportunities for Latina/o artists" so that UrbanTheater could provide "a strong mentorship foundation for those just starting." Elisa Marina Alvarado imagined Teatro Visión becoming a leading laboratorio for new Latina/o work, which would cultivate a practice of "artistic development in collaboration with the community." Josefina López conjured a future for Casa 0101 that would "reflect the community" and "be the place where people see their possibilities" (while also being the anchor of "a theater row in the barrio"). "I want there to be a ton of theater companies that are all trying to take on the story of being human, [to] transcend all the things that make us different, really look at what frightens us. That's my dream."

Other dreams addressed visions of organizational transformation. Jacob Padrón dreamed a "very simple" dream of the day when a Latina/o artist would be invited to become a member of Steppenwolf's ensemble. Aurora Theatre's Anthony Rodriguez hoped to "make our organization look more like our community." Marissa Chibas hoped to help build stronger international collaborations so that co-created art might build bridges and find power in a larger community. Teatro Luna's Alex Meda imagined "the dreams of the women currently, formerly, and futurely at Luna." Patricia Ybarra imagined a future in which the "corporatization of the university that especially exploits non-tenured and non-permanent faculty" would be stopped, alongside one in which no student could earn a bachelor's, master's, or doctoral degree without having read or performed a Latina/o play.

Some visions considered the fortification of the infrastructure necessary to share their organization's legacy with and for future organizations. Alberto Justiano said simply, "I want to leave a legacy," as he expressed his "wish to have a stable theater with a [sustainable] budget [so] that I can pass the keys to some young whippersnapper Latina/o that can take it to the next level." Tiffany Vega dreamed of the day HI-ARTS would "have a staff of no less than twenty" as well as an unlimited budget, its own theater, and a path-breaking curriculum, while also "employing our elders [and] giving them health insurance" so that hip hop would be "given its due as an art form and as a culture." Rose Portillo of About Productions expressed the "real simple, basic dream" of having her ensemble's self-generated work adapted into a collection of published scripts so that the company's repertoire might be read, restaged, and appreciated by other groups, and not remain wholly "dependent on [About Productions] producing them." Most speakers in the inner circle, in one way or another, shared Su Teatro's Tony Garcia's desire "to get ahead of some of this shit" and "to really start to work with our organizations to build an infrastructure long-term."

Once the microphone had been passed around the entire inner circle, voices from the outer circles began to offer their visions for the future. Freelance director José Carrasquillo conjured a "guerilla theater" action that would stage a rolling, national reading festival of new plays. To which playwright and producer Caridad Svich replied, "I'm actually doing that!" Svich then described the idea behind her 30/30 initiative, that invited writers to share their works "laterally" with interested groups ("universities, colleges, student groups, coffee houses, bands of actors in their living rooms or garages, higher structures, lower structures"), all to permit readings of contemporary Latina/o plays "to create a different type of dialogue around the work."

Ricardo Gutierrez, the artistic director of Chicago's Teatro Vista, shared his dream of repurposing a vacant grocery store as a cultural center. Rose Cano spoke about Seattle's eSe Teatro's work staging bilingual play readings in homeless shelters and imagined sharing the work as a national model. Teresa Marrero proposed "the notion of the enlightened scholar" as she thought toward the moment when she no longer would "hear *teatros* say that 'we don't have qualified critics talking about our work.'" Playwright Maria Alexandria Beech reflected on the ways certain European MFA programs were integrating coursework in entrepreneurship within arts training programs. "If we start thinking of training [young Latinas/os] to be producers," Beech observed, "this whole landscape could change." Director/actor/educator Richard Perez stated simply, "I look forward to the day when we no longer have to have these convenings."

Abel López then noted,

> So we can see that our dreams are not unlimited [but] that they are very expansive. But on the flip side, what are some of the challenges that you face? And in thinking about those challenges, we can talk about both those challenges that are internal to us and systemic challenges as well. … We also want to hear from you about what models you may already be using to address such challenges.

"I always say that Su Teatro never sold out because nobody ever made an offer." —Tony Garcia

What followed was a searching conversation about the pressures placed upon Latina/o artists and arts organizations to provide bold leadership within their communities, even as they also remain reliant on those same communities for economic and other support. Reflecting on the artistic success and community impact of Casa 0101's "Brown and Out" festival (a series dedicated to homophobia and heterosexism within immigrant and other communities in East Los Angeles), Josefina López ruminated on the potential implications of seeking foundation funding for Casa 0101, a community-based theater. "At what point do we sell out," she asked, "because we need to fund shows people won't come to see?"

"I always say that Su Teatro never sold out because nobody ever made an offer," quipped Tony Garcia, Artistic Director of Denver's long-standing Su Teatro. *[Guffaws from the crowd]* Garcia followed with a serious philosophical question about the nature of artistic leadership: "Do we move forward by pushing or pulling the cart? [...] That's the dynamic we have in a lot of our organizations. We're trying to get through Saturday and we have no idea what the next month looks like. How do we get ahead of the cart and then pull what's behind us?"

Tiffany Vega next raised the challenge that comes when one is "the only Latina/o in the room." Vega drew the connection between the legacies of Reaganomics and practices by big theater companies that send "teaching artists, who are people of color, and they send them out to these inner-city schools… and then these kids come to these theaters… and they don't see these teaching artists on these stages." As a result,

Vega argued, the major theaters were exploiting artists of color for funding and publicity, without committing meaningfully to diversification of the arts. "You use us," Vega said, "but you don't produce us." Vega continued, "The reason I got into producing is that I got sick and tired of people saying that we're not being produced because we're not producers, or we're not decision-makers, or we're not sitting at the table." Alberto Justiano emphasized the importance of having "someone there to create the infrastructure so that art can be made." He observed that, "one of the reasons so many theaters fail" is that "there wasn't the one person lifting the infrastructure… to continue on beyond the ten years when people are excited." Reflecting on his own path, Justiano affirmed that "I never went to school for theater management, and I made a lot of mistakes… and it would have been a lot easier to have somebody who knew what they were doing so we didn't repeat the mistakes of the past."

Conversation continued to raise particular points of challenge for contemporary Latina/o theatermakers. Maria Alexandria Beech spoke to the debilitating effects, both creatively and professionally, of "the reading" as a primary mechanism of new work development. Marissa Chibas raised the importance and difficulty of identifying those institutions that are worthy and welcoming collaborators. And Rose Portillo opened the question that would guide the next cycle of conversation when she commented on the challenges of working in a historical moment in which "we don't have the cultural pride in giving to arts organizations anymore." Portillo put the challenge to the room: "How do we begin to make it valuable again to the business community, to see that it's a feather in their cap to be associated with arts organizations and art-making?"

Moderator Abel López amplified Portillo's challenge to the wider circle: "Is it also a challenge to make a value proposition to our own communities?" López pressed the group to consider the challenge of communicating the "value of the art or the value of our organizations" within the Latina/o community.

The next few speakers spoke directly to the "value proposition" of Latina/o arts. "One of the mistakes that we make when we approach people about money," Su Teatro's Tony Garcia observed,

> *is that we have a tendency to say "I need this" and "I need that." … When you sell things to people, you don't go to them and say, "I want you to buy this couch because I'll get more money out of it." … The reason you do it is because it's about you. Here's what you get. You get to sit on the couch. You get to lie down. Your kids get to have their stories told. … That's the mistake I think we make so often is we think it's about us. And so long as we make it about us, you're going to keep asking.*

Next, Elisa Marina Alvarado spoke about the importance of building "an ongoing relationship of social value to our community." Anthony Rodriguez added that the business community might not care about the art itself, but rather "the success you are creating" with and through the art. "They will buy into that," Rodriguez affirmed, "They really will." Teatro Luna's Alex Meda emphasized the importance of looking to the audience first and the funders second. "How are we cultivating our audiences, and how are we keeping them engaged in our conversations?" Meda affirmed,

"I believe it starts there, because that's what our funders will listen to."

Patricia Ybarra offered perhaps a contrary point of view: "As theater educators and sometimes as artists, we're forced into models of entrepreneurship that constantly ask us [not only] to argue for our own validity, but also to try to fit ourselves into the economic models of risk that actually give you one chance, and then you're done, and you're out if you don't make it." Ybarra cautioned that rushing to make art "worth the risk" actually encouraged the downscaling of the kind of "long-term collaborative modes of art-making" that so many in the room were dreaming toward. She then encouraged the group to "to quit unabashedly and uncritically adopting that language" of business and science and remaking "themselves in the mold of something they are not" because, in so doing, artists might well be, however inadvertently, setting themselves up to fail.

Jacob Padrón next spoke in praise of mentorship.

I feel like the people who taught me how to be a producer are in this room, so I want to offer that up, as an affirmation, the value of mentorship and the people who saw something in me that I didn't see in myself. …I hope, as we exist in community over the weekend, that we continue to shine that light on people we believe in.

Moderator Abel López then posed a provocative question: "As we see a more diversified America, is there a need for Latina/o theaters?"

The first voices to speak answered with a resounding "*Yes!*" Josefina López reminded those assembled that "if I didn't have my own theater company, I wouldn't have a career as a playwright," adding that "I wish we didn't need Latina/o theaters but, until that happens…" Su Teatro's Tony Garcia reflected on his company's experience performing in a large regional house. "They loved being there," Garcia recalled, "and I said the master invited you to visit the house. He did not invite you to move in. …We have to control our houses." Cara Mía's David Lozano also spoke up affirming that it remained important for independent companies to "determine how we tell our stories and how we create and establish our own artistic processes." Next, scholar Brian Herrera reminded those assembled that "area studies and ethnic studies, Latina/o studies, Chicana/o studies programs are being phased out" throughout higher education because "there's this idea that they can now be part of the survey." Herrera continued, "If there is a theater in the future, you bet they'll be doing Ibsen; you bet they'll be doing Shakespeare; you bet they'll be continuing certain traditions." Herrera encouraged those assembled to "continue the deep dive into the depth and the breadth and the full dimension of Latina/o literary and theatrical expression" because "we need that depth of inquiry, we need that breadth of voices, we need that diversity of form."

Actor/playwright Christopher de Paola offered a somewhat contrary view, questioning the "idea of segregationist theater" and "whether we're trying to protect something." De Paola asked, "How important is it for us to be protectionist? And is it hurting us at the same time, because we're segregating ourselves, saying we're off on the side doing this."

Diane Rodriguez then challenged the room: "How do we as powerful people figure out how we live in this current reality from a powerful position?" Rodriguez continued, "I love my position. I'm a leader. Not necessarily leading a Chicano organization, but I am a Chicana and I am leading from all that I bring to the table from all these years." Rodriguez continued, "It's not about selling out; it's not about giving up; it's about approaching all of it. [...] Can we lead the diversity/inclusion conversation by showing how it's done?"

The next round of speakers echoed Rodriguez's challenge. José Luis Valenzuela affirmed that "the most important part of the work again is quality; funders are going to come to you if they like what you are doing." Clyde Valentín affirmed the importance of "recognizing our power and our work." Valentín encouraged all assembled to "embrace scale" as he reflected on an artist's admonition to "let it burn and let it grow. Some things are going to burn down," Valentín agreed, "and all of that has to happen to move forward."

In response to a query received via Twitter, Abel López then asked the group to name "some alternative models that don't force us to be what we're not." In the few minutes remaining, the group discussed several models, including crowd funding, in which a foundation or angel matches the crowd sourced funding; the L3C tax designation, presently available only in a few states, which simplifies tax procedures for investing in projects that are socially beneficial while also being commercial; and strategies for making service on artistic boards attractive to the most wealthy and most qualified members of the Latina/o community.

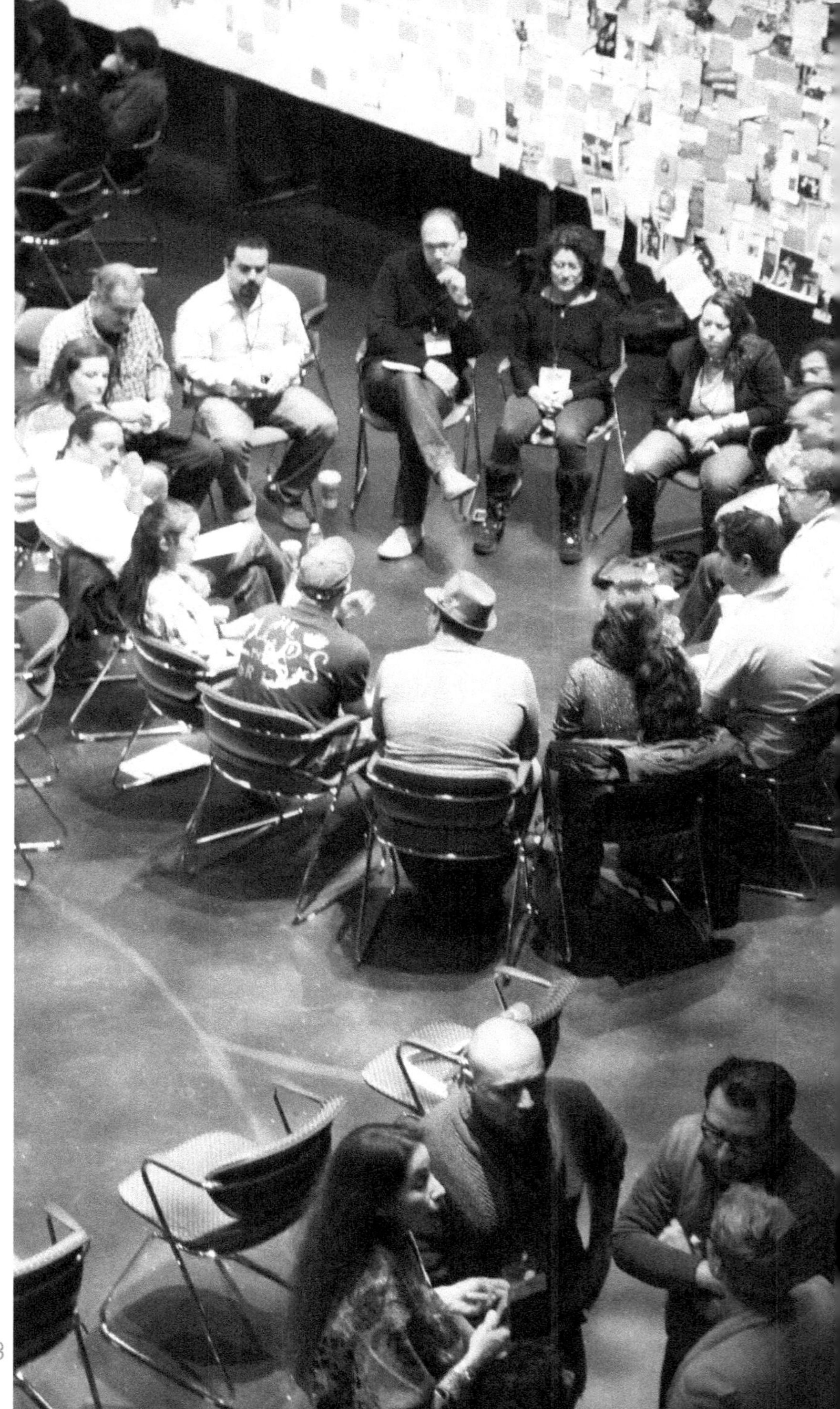

The Conocimiento Groups

For the third and final session of the day, the co-facilitators invited participants to reconvene and continue the conversation begun by their *conocimiento* group earlier that day. The co-facilitators prompted participants to distill their thoughts based on their own perspectives as well as what they had heard throughout the day. The facilitators also asked each group to prepare a report that might convey to the larger group the modes of strategic thinking each *conocimiento* group had explored.

Not quite an hour later, co-facilitator Clyde Valentín brought the group back together to share their *conocimiento* reports in preparation for the work of the following day. Reminding all that he would be enforcing a strict five-minute time limit for each presentation, Valentín also quoted, without attribution, some phrases he overheard during the final group meetings:

Anglo Western theater is Arthur Miller, Tennessee Williams, and those other guys.

People go to the movies and do all these things. I mean how much do people spend on soccer?

Hopefully, when I'm too old for this, there are ten other people willing to do it.

Valentín welcomed the first *conocimiento* group to the area of the room immediately in front of the colorful timeline. The presentations that took to this makeshift stage arrived in the form of choreopoems and raps, manifestos and proclamations. Some presentations were more embodied than others, but all ultimately engaged the rhetorics of performance to distill their *conocimiento*'s conversation. The following account describes each presentation, and offers an embedded summary of the ways each group's morning and afternoon conversations informed their final performance/presentation.

Conocimiento Group 1

The first *conocimiento* group brought together those participants affiliated with major regional or LORT theaters. This group included Christopher Acebo, Lydia Garcia, Melinda Lopez, Jacob Padrón, Diane Rodriguez, Tanya Saracho, Stephanie Ybarra, and Karen Zacarías.

Jacob Padrón reported on his group's "robust conversation" regarding regional theaters, noting that a recurring image in the conversation was that of "the castle on the hill." As Padrón named the image, Melinda raised her arms above her head, creating a visual embodiment of the edifice of that castle on that hill. Padrón affirmed that the "castle" image proved to be a guiding one for the group's wide-ranging conversation about the ways in which the individual artists negotiated the relationship between doing their work and their desire to be welcomed within "the castle." Yet, at the same time, Padrón noted that even as the individuals in the group discussed the ways in which they were constantly analyzing their value within these institutions, they acknowledged their shared impulse to shift the institutional paradigm.

This central tension—the desire to be part of the institution colliding with the desire to transform it—guided the group's conversation from its first gathering early that morning, when the group offered a concentrated assessment of the institution, especially when viewed from the outside, to the first *conocimiento* group of the afternoon. Two primary themes emerged. First, the idea of "the season" stirred observations about inconsistent efforts toward inclusion, limited notions of what Latina/o stories might be, and the persistent lack of awareness within regional theaters regarding the depth and diversity of skilled, available Latina/o talent in all disciplines. Second, the group contemplated the role of decision-makers, especially artistic directors: their predisposition toward certain kinds of Latina/o work; the pressures that made them especially risk averse and inclined toward "confirmed" successes; and their inclination to "downsize" Latina/o work and produce it on a limited scale. Throughout, the group considered the myriad problems stemming from an over reliance on "the pipeline" or the established routes through which decision-makers identified creative personnel for opportunities available within their organizations.

As they reconvened later in the day for their second *conocimiento* conversation, the group assessed whether the rhetoric of inclusion and exclusion was the most illuminating or effective. Conversation soon turned toward whether and how institutions might be changed from within, as well as through strategic alliances with artists beyond the "castle walls." In this second conversation, the group explored how mutual advocacy might serve both individual artists and larger institutions. In particular, the group discussed the artist's need to think selfishly (what's best for my work, how do I pay the bills) at the same time strategically (how might my contributions guide the institution, how can I support allies within and beyond the institution). The group quickly agreed that advocacy and mentorship were perhaps the most essential strategies in leveraging the institution's resources in support of one's own work and on behalf of Latina/o theatermakers in all areas of production and at all career levels. Additionally, the group agreed that cultivating Latinas/os as legible arts leaders (in areas other than arts outreach and education) was crucial to expanding the diversity of voices "in the room" for key decisions of all sorts (including but not limited to hiring, marketing, audience outreach, and crafting mission statements).

Throughout their time together, the group encountered the persistent necessity for critiquing hierarchical institutional structures and sustaining grassroots and independent theater work beyond the institution. Seeking to move consciously away from an adversarial model that situates some organizations as "haves" and others as "have nots," the group developed a "both/and" approach. Here, participants hoped to resist the discourse of scarcity as they considered how differences in resources might be understood as contributing to a healthy "ecosystem." The ecosystem model, the group hoped, might both amplify the urgency of cultivating healthy and mutual relationships among larger and smaller organizations and strengthen the connective tissues among organizations. Such a model might permit Latina/o theatermakers to happily and productively leverage their access to the larger institutions, as well as the Latina/o community and the broader network of Latina/o theater artists, all while valuing the artist's and the institution's rootedness in the smaller, often community-based theaters, as crucial components of the theater ecosystem.

In presenting the work of their *conocimiento* collaboration to the larger assembly, artists in the major regional or LORT theaters group decided to offer a declaration. Members of the group each offered a declaration beginning with the word "whereas," and as each speaker began, Tanya Saracho raised a large, hand-lettered sign upon which the word "whereas" appeared in hand-drawn bubble letters.

KAREN ZACARÍAS

Whereas we realize that we are the protagonists of our own lives, that we are the lead characters of our own story, that America is shifting. We are no longer the maid photobombing in the background. We are moving to the center and we need to own that.

MELINDA LOPEZ

Whereas it is healthy and good for playwrights to aspire to be part of the American Theater canon; and Whereas it is healthy and good for the designers and directors and theatermakers of all stripes in the Latina/o world to aspire to be represented in the regional theater; and Whereas it is healthy and good to know as an early career artist, as a mid-career artist, or as a late-career artist that you will leave your legacy for those that come beyond and behind you.

STEPHANIE YBARRA

Whereas we believe the Latina/o theater community is a thriving community, and actually has a healthy ecology, representative of individual artists and institutions; Whereas we believe we have powerful origin stories, individually and collectively, and the extent to which we are naming those stories, saying them loudly and saying them often, is the extent to which we are going to build that legacy and forge that path ahead. For example …

TANYA SARACHO

There wouldn't be an Evelina Fernandez without a Teatro Esperanza; there wouldn't be a Diane Rodriguez or Kinan Valdez without El Teatro Campesino; there wouldn't be a Chris Acebo without Cornerstone; there wouldn't be a Richard Montoya without Culture Clash; there wouldn't be a Cándido Tirado without Repertorio Espanol; there wouldn't be Abel López without GALA Hispanic; and there wouldn't be a Tanya Saracho without Teatro Luna!

As the crowd burst into cheers and applause, Stephanie Ybarra offered a concluding thought. "We focused a lot on what we do have, celebrating the tools we do have. …The truth is we have the tools to build whatever castle or whatever house we want to go forward."

Conocimiento Group 2

The second *conocimiento* group gathered those affiliated primarily with community-based or culturally-specific theater groups. This group included Elisa Marina Alvarado, Sandra Delgado, Ricardo Gutierrez, Alberto Justiano, Josefina López, Nancy García Loza, David Lozano, Sandra Marquez, Lou Moreno, Marcos Nájera, Mark David Pinate Anthony Rodriguez, Ivan Vega, and Tiffany Vega.

Tony Garcia prefaced the group's presentation with a brief statement. "We had a very interesting, rambling discussion. Marketing. Development. Networking. Kind of everything in the whole world about our world." Garcia noted that the group came up with a "metaphor" that they would present "in a very physical way to you." Garcia then invited those assembled to hum or sing the melody to "*La Marcha de Zacatecas*," a Mexican patriotic song often used in wedding or other community dances. "So!" Garcia shouted, "One! Two! Three!" *[Spirited singing]*

The metaphor of "*la marcha*" might be seen in the *conocimiento's* first conversation, as each contributor offered, in turn, an introduction to his or her work by answering the question, "How did we get involved in theater?" As each individual spoke, the group began to name a series of looping themes that connected them to one another. For many, theater's attraction derived from its potential to conjure community through art alongside its capacity to manifest critical dialogues and networks of support. Many in the group spoke of the powerful ways theater can build community through the act of communal creation. At the same time, the group spoke persistently about the challenges of sustaining community engagement, even and especially within a theater dedicated to that community. This led to conversation about the paradoxical challenges, both artistic and administrative, that emerge when a community-based theater seeks to engage audiences and others (especially funders) from beyond the community. Throughout, the group contemplated the pivot of community and engagement as a fulcrum of power for their theaters.

> The group contemplated the pivot of community and engagement as a fulcrum of power for their theaters.

As they reconvened later in the day, the group noted that it was "both comforting and depressing" that organizations at all levels seemed to struggle with the same problems (funding, facilities, staffing, audiences). The group also reflected on the impulse to complain about scarcity, as if access to more resources would be the source and solution to all problems, perhaps as a way to avoid more difficult conversations about the organization itself. The group considered several particular problems: how to identify and educate funders, large and small; how to balance the principles of accessibility and openness (which often mean free or subsidized tickets) with the proposition that Latina/o theater is valuable and deserving of monetary support from the community;

how to connect the willingness of Latina/o audiences to spend money on entertainment to the practice of participating in community-based arts; and finally, the imperative that community-based Latina/o theater artists remain in conversation with their colleagues in other kinds of theater. Throughout, the conversation returned to the challenge of accessing resources (money and time) and developing and sustaining an infrastructure for a company's ongoing initiatives, including national collaborations and exchanges.

The group members concluded that their work might be best communicated to the larger group through a physical staging of their vision for a large community circle that would enable networking and sharing of artistic resources, while also providing support to other artists and organizations.

As its presentation began, the community-based and culturally-specific *conocimiento* group invited the support of the larger assembly by first asking everyone to add their voices and handclaps as the musical underscoring for the group's marcha.

Josefina López began the marcha by stepping forward and shouting a single word ("Networking!") before stepping to one side, her back to the audience. Next, Alberto Justiano proclaimed another single word ("Sharing!") as he moved to face López. The two then raised their arms high and joined hands. Mark David Pinate then hollered "Value!" before stepping under the arch now created by López and Justiano's joined hands. As Pinate stepped to stand at López's side, Marcos Nájera shouted another "Passion!" and stepped through the arch still configured by Justiano and López's joined hands. Taking his place next to Justiano, Nájera and Pinate raised and joined their hands to create the next link in the arch. In the moments that followed, each of the *conocimiento* group's fourteen members shouted a word into the air—Inspiration! EastLA! *Pocha Nostra!*—as they first moved through the arch and then joined as its next link.

Once all the members of the *conocimiento* group had moved through and joined the arch, members placed their hands on the shoulders of the person immediately in front. As they continued to sing the refrain of "*La Marcha de Zacatecas*," and as those gathered continued to clap in rhythm, the group performers stepped their newly configured circle in a gentle rotation, placed their arms across each other's shoulders, and then turned the circle inward, and then outward according the pulsing rhythm of handclaps. The circle raised its collective voice to proclaim, "*Pasion unida!*"

"Our goal was to create culturally competent audiences for all our theaters. We had a few ways we thought that could happen." —Patricia Ybarra

Conocimiento Group 3

The third *conocimiento* group gathered those theatermakers affiliated with academic institutions or scholarly enterprises, with most contributors holding full-time positions at a range of public and private universities. This group included Marissa Chibas, Micha Espinosa, Brian Herrera, Jorge Huerta, Tiffany Ana López, Teresa Marrero, Irma Mayorga, Noe Montez, Richard Perez, Beatriz Rizk, Bernardo Solano, and Patricia Ybarra.

Patricia Ybarra framed the primary goal emerging from the *conocimiento* conversation: "Our goal was to create culturally competent audiences for all our theaters. We had a few ways we thought that could happen."

The morning's conversation among the scholars began with professional introductions, with members of the group detailing how their work on campus as theater scholars and/or practitioners (performer, playwright, dramaturg, director) operated within the academic apparatus of teaching, research, and publishing. The group agreed that the increased visibility of Latina/o theater and performance scholars and their scholarship were impressive. More Latina/o theater faculty are earning tenure, and Latina/o theater faculty across the country are pioneering innovative curricular practices, often with innovative partnerships both on campus and within communities beyond it. The group noted that a Latina is the next president of the largest academic theater organization, and another holds an endowed chair. At the same time, the group acknowledged that the university remains a difficult, even hostile, place for Latina/o theatermakers to work. The increased pressure upon faculty to accomplish much more, within the same (or greatly restricted) limits, places a special burden on Latina/o faculty in the arts. The group members expressed concern that many Latina/o faculty in university theater departments are expected to maintain full profiles as both scholars and artists, even as they encounter entrenched resistance among their colleagues regarding the legitimacy of Latina/o theater. They acknowledged that too few Latina/o faculty teach in the areas of acting, directing, and design, while also noting that theater departments persistently fail to actively recruit and retain Latina/o students for their courses or their productions. Schools remain slow to integrate courses on Latina/o theater into the curriculum, a fact that contributes to a general lack of exposure to and experience with Latina/o theater among both students and faculty, and continues to produce audiences and theatermakers without even the most rudimentary cultural competence to appreciate the complexity and contribution of Latina/o theater of the last fifty years (let alone the last five hundred). Thus, the advocacy for all aspects of Latina/o theater falls as an additional burden upon the small number of Latina/o faculty in the still comparatively few places they hold permanent positions.

Reconvening after the listening sessions, the scholars embraced their own responsibility for the field's failure in making the long history of Latina/o theater available to other scholars, to Latina/o theatermakers, and to audiences. There emerged a passionate consensus that the time was right to document this long and complex history, perhaps through a multi-tiered publication strategy, which might address both general readers and specialists. At the same time, the group affirmed the importance of advocating for theatermaking beyond the field, especially as a component of educational success. Noting the absence of Theater for Young Audience scholars at the Convening, the group emphasized the importance of innovative educational partnerships with K-12 educators as essential to the valuing of Latina/o theater within the academy, within the field, and beyond. As conversation resolved, the group affirmed how important it was to name the ongoing pressures and challenges faced by university-affiliated Latina/o theatermakers. At the same time, the group recognized that academically-affiliated theatermakers must work to cultivate culturally competent theatermakers among both university students and university faculty. The group hopes such scholars might also develop strategies to leverage university resources in ways that might help sustain Latina/o artists and organizations, while also expanding the cultural and theatrical literacy of university theater departments and their students.

With her fellow scholars forming a single line behind her, Patricia Ybarra distilled the group's work:

As most of us are primarily educators, we are interested in education on every spectrum, inside our institutions and outside of them.

So that doesn't just mean that we are educating our students, but also means educating our colleagues [and] also creating bridges to community.

Our second goal was to create dynamic modes of using university resources to help and nurture working artists in a number of different ways, whether that is in terms of production [or] in terms of us being competent critics—a model of scholar as patron.

Looking at the timeline behind us, we want to be sure that we have a Latina/o theater history for everyone. For those of you who don't know this, there are a number of different radicalized and minoritarian groups that have a narrative history of their theater. And Latina/o theater history doesn't really have that narrative history.

So what we're talking about is making sure that we can write a narrative that archives our history and that is accessible for everyone. Moving five hundred years back before the 1960s, we were creating performance in this country. One thing that we are really dedicated to is moving five hundred years back. That forces us to acknowledge indigenous and African roots in our performance culture.

At this moment, the scholars, inspired by their role in spreading awareness of the timeline behind them, improvised a spontaneous, awkward and brief kick line, which was indulged with cheers and applause from the those assembled. "This was not rehearsed," Jorge reminded the group. Bernardo Solano added, "We work with our brains!"

Conocimiento Group 4

The fourth *conocimiento* group was the first of two to gather independent artists, including those who identified as playwrights, directors, actors, educators, administrators, or some combination thereof. This group included José Carrasquillo, Christopher DePaola, Georgina H. Escobar, Amparo Garcia-Crow, Anne García-Romero, Matthew Paul Olmos, Rose Portillo, Elaine Romero, Tony Sonera, Cándido Tirado, and Enrique Urueta.

The group gathered onstage to form a wide semi-circle, open to the audience. At the semi-circle's center stood Anne García-Romero, microphone in hand.

The independent artists in this group dedicated the morning conversation to the exchange of brief biographical self-portraits describing the experience of becoming involved in theater. These narratives of unanticipated encounter and youthful discovery developed several themes: theater as a means of reconciling abiding questions of community and collaboration; engaging the politics of Latina/o life and experience in the United States; and generating work in conversation and community. Throughout, the group discussed what it meant to be Latina/o storytellers who have adopted theater as their mode and medium for telling tales.

As they gathered again after the listening sessions, the group dove immediately into the challenges of identity and the way those challenges played out for individual artists and for organizations. For the group, the persistent question of "Who are we?" proved to be both necessary and its own problem ("like a dog chasing its tail"). As they contemplated the challenges of diversity and inclusivity, the conversation celebrated the complexity of Latina/o identity ("there's no uniformity within *Latinidad*"). Yet, for all the potential inclusivity of *Latinidad*,

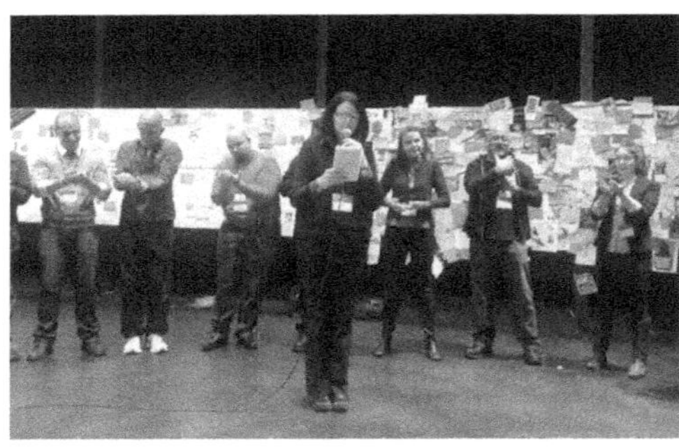

the group expressed frustration with what felt like invisible obstacles causing Latina/o exclusion from theater in the United States. The artists wondered whether that exclusion stemmed from who occupied positions of power or from the practices of exclusivity that defines theater itself (traditions, institutions, canons). They also questioned whether seeking inclusion was the most worthy goal, inquiring about how Latinas/os might move forward without leaving themselves behind. As they ruminated on the peculiar practices of segregation that persist in the professional theater, they also affirmed the potential of *Latinidad* to model an alternate paradigm. They concluded with the question that would guide their presentation: How do we take the experience and practice of inclusivity that guides us as Latina/o people, and as Latina/o artists, back to our theaters, communities, and schools?

In their group presentation, Anne García-Romero stood at the center of a semi-circle created by her colleagues. Georgina H. Escobar stood at one end, wearing a clown nose. As García-Romero spoke each word or phrase into the microphone, the group offered a gestural response:

Identity ... Inclusivity ... [The group behind her raises their hands to shoulder level, with their palms open toward themselves. They then repeatedly flip their palms outward and then inward again.] *Inclusivity.* [The group raises their hands upward as though to catch something. They then bring their hands downward, cradling something in their hands that they regard with kindness, with care, with pride, with curiosity.] *Financial support. [In an instant, all members of the group begin reaching outward, first grasping at what might be there and then eyeing or pointing at each other with acquisitive interest.] How do we move forward without leaving ourselves behind?* [Group members link their thumbs together to suggest a bird or butterfly winging up and away.] *The importance of dreams.* [Each member of the group pivots to bring their flying hands back toward the center. The group, with big smiles, moves from the stage.]

Conocimiento Group 5

The fifth group also constituted a gathering of independent artists, including those who identified as playwrights, directors, actors, educators, administrators, or some combination thereof. This group included Luis Alfaro, Maria Alexandria Beech, Juliette Carrillo, Migdalia Cruz, Regina García, Marisela Treviño Orta, Lisa Portes, Tlaloc Rivas, Jerry Ruiz, Octavio Solis, and Laurie Woolery.

The group gathered onstage in a long line. Lisa Portes took the microphone.

We are the individual artists and, if you take a look at the group of people we have up here, you can imagine that we had quite an intense conversation the entire time. …Perhaps one of the most intense moments that I will take from this entire experience.

In response to the question, "How did you fall into the theater?" the members of this group described variously transformative encounters with the form during their youth. Some recalled deep engagement with other literary or visual arts; others remembered school or community networks that solicited their involvement; and some detailed how an accident of circumstance revealed theater as a personal or creative path. For some, these encounters were mundane; for others, encounters came through profound experiences of activism or trauma. As the conversation moved to the question of what was and was not working, these mostly mid-career artists spoke of the challenges of sustaining oneself, both creatively and materially, through the ups, the downs, and especially the plateaus that characterize a career in the arts. Some commented upon the constant pressure to reinvent oneself; several pointed to work as university teaching faculty for providing a measure of stability; and others pointed to community engagement as an especially sustaining kind of work. Several nodded to the temptations of leaving theater altogether, perhaps to work in film or television, or to develop fiction rather than plays.

When pressed to identify what needed to change, suggestions spilled forth but soon found a particular theme: how to develop an effective diversity of strategies at all levels of an organization's operation. The group spoke emphatically of the imperative of diversity within creative personnel but also beyond it, noting the importance of diversity at the audience level, at the level of the board of directors, and in volunteer/intern structures (especially those charged with reviewing submissions from playwrights, actors, and others). The group expressed an interest in developing holistic diversity strategies that integrated diversity as a value throughout the organization and hoped that such efforts might somehow both sustain and serve the Latina/o artists working within those organizations.

The group returned from the listening sessions with a deep sense of obligation that was balanced by a profound ambivalence. The artists were wary of the peculiar pressures placed on Latina/o artists to represent themselves, their ancestors, and their communities. In discussion about the ways that Latina/o artists might help bridge persistent divides, they felt an excitement about the opportunity for Latina/o artists to embody the kind of inclusivity and diversity they craved. This strategy seemed especially apt for mid-career artists who might have the opportunity (and feel the obligation) to bridge generations and communities as one way of charting a dynamic continuum among Latina/o theatermakers at all levels. At the same time, some in the group expressed concern that, by being representatives and ambassadors, the pressure to "whitewash" (or make one's story acceptable to non-Latina/o groups) carried its own costs. As the group resolved their conversation, they sought a balance of these pressures within the metaphor animated by the convening itself, the idea that each person present in the room was, in effect, not merely an individual but a delegate for a broad range of constituencies. The group asked: How can we enact the role of delegate to preserve and honor our history as a living legacy? How can we carry that legacy forward in championing our own work (and that of other artists) at all times? How, as delegates, might we resist the sometimes self-sabotaging strategies of "stealth" subversion and infiltration and advocate more forcefully that Latinas/os have a rightful place at the center of all aspects of theatermaking?

How can we enact the role of delegate to preserve and honor our history as a living legacy? How can we carry that legacy forward in championing our own work (and that of other artists) at all-times?

Lisa Portes spoke on behalf of the group:

It was three things that we focused on. … The first is that we are passionate about the fact that our story is the American story, [and] that we need to recognize that there is a paradigm shift that's occurring right now; that it's time to own our power and to find power in ourselves as delegates to the larger community; and [that it's time] to honor our art [and] be our mainstream. We are the American story, and we need that story.

Second, we are intergenerational, and we wanted to talk about how we had to build bridges across generations, honoring those that came in the beginnings, at least according to this timeline [Gesturing behind her] and recognizing the wounds, the scars. How can we reach back and honor los veteranos [and] heal them? And how can the master playwrights stay in long enough so that people coming up can recognize that there is room for us all?

And we talked a lot about the conflict between gentle subversion and self-sabotage—that now is the moment to form friendships and alliances to subvert organizational structures, and to recognize [that] now is the moment to take power.

At this moment, Lisa Portes surprised her colleagues by saying, "With that I'm going to ask each of the artists in this line to mention one word that comes from their heart, that came from our conversation." Luis Alfaro gently pressed Marisela Treviño Orta to the microphone.

MARISELA TREVIÑO ORTA Delegate. Noun form.
LUIS ALFARO I was gonna say improv. But it's actually Legacy.
MIGDALIA CRUZ Family.

REGINA GARCÍA Home.

LAURIE WOOLERY Work.

JULIETTE CARRILLO Belonging.

OCTAVIO SOLIS Ancestors.

TLALOC RIVAS Love.

ALEX BEECH Sanctity.

JERRY RUIZ Responsibility.

LISA PORTES Thank you very much.

Conocimiento Group 6

The sixth *conocimiento* group gathered those involved in international collaborations and included a sizable number of producers and administrators. Among them were Kevin Becerra, Rose Cano, Evelina Fernandez, Olga Garay-English, Daniel Jáquez, Alex Meda, Mario Ernesto Sánchez, and Caridad Svich.

Mario Ernesto Sánchez stepped forward, to offer an unanticipated prefatory announcement. "I have to confess to you," Sánchez began, "That I had a very boring group. We didn't have much to rehearse, but we talked a lot and we argued a lot." Sánchez gestured to Kevin Becerra's notepad. "And the conclusions are right here," Sánchez continued, "And now, after he's finished talking to you, we're all going to say at one time: Cuba!" *[Room erupts in laughter]*

Kevin Becerra observed, "I will tell you I learned more about Miami today than I ever thought I would, thanks to Mario Ernesto. …What a beautiful country it is! *[Crowd laughter]* Becerra continued, "Here's our boring report from our boring group! We actually had a really great conversation that was very robust."

The morning's conversation among those involved in international collaborations began with professional introductions, with an emphasis on the interplay between each contributor's individual journey and his or her institutional biography. As the introductions proceeded, several themes emerged. Some commented on how an individual's priorities can shift an organization's orientation toward national and transnational networks of collaboration. Others described how they sought a sense of meaningful interconnection with other individuals, collaborators, and organizations in defiance of geographical distance. Several spoke about their commitment to making sensible, strategic use of existing available resources (including undervalued resources like community partners), and others spoke of how national and international networks can be fortified through presenting the work of theater partners from other regions and introducing worthy artists to new audiences. Throughout, the contributors expressed an abiding awareness of the burden of advocating for international work in the United States in tandem with the opportunity to exploit theater's power to open conversations about globalization.

A mix of anxiety and frustration kicked off the second session, regarding both the guiding premise of the Convening as well as its anticipated purpose and results. Two clusters of questions in particular absorbed the group's interest. First, is the Convening concerned with Latina/o personnel and content for our stages? Or is it about telling our stories with the worthiest collaborators, irrespective of their cultural background? Aren't our professional frustrations shared by most theater artists? What's the point of focusing so emphatically on what's different for Latinas/os? Next, the group wondered whether and how this Convening might have a meaningful impact, given that the problems named at the last gathering in 1986 were the same we're naming today ("I wonder if thirty years from now, we're going to be talking about the same problems.")

In response to these anxieties, the group affirmed several principles of purpose that the Convening might provide those in attendance:

First, the value of spaces like the Convening to move beyond a position of self-defense and self-affirmation as artists and organizations and toward a critical engagement with how to produce artists and leaders who are competent, well-trained, and thoroughly-versed in the national and international scene. The Convening and the LTC have the potential to serve as a think tank for Latina/o theater advocacy, as well as a venue for sharing skills and stories of success and struggle, all of which might help constituent organizations fortify their infrastructure.

Second, the arts economy is prone to a cult of personality, where certain individuals or particular organizations draw all the attention and all the resources. Gatherings like this one emphasize the strength and insight to be found in consortium, while also acknowledging how central the practices of ensemble, community-building, and community partnerships are to the work of many Latina/o theater artists and organizations. Our differences are actually more visible in gatherings like this, even though we're gathered because of what we ostensibly share. This Convening models an alternate approach to community building—across generational, geographic, cultural, and institutional differences—that places us not in competition, but in collaboration.

Third, because of the widely acknowledged facts of individual burnout and organizational collapse, gatherings like this one force intergenerational communications and encourage collective strategies so as to not waste energy, replicate work, or place ourselves in unproductive competition. If we do not create the occasions that force communication across generational, regional, and institutional divides, we will still be confronting the same problems in thirty years. We need opportunities like this Convening to develop a meaningful sense of continuity and longevity, as well as a broader sense of "institutional memory" for Latina/o not-for-profit theater in the United States.

In addition to these guiding principles, the group also noted a constellation of pressing concerns regarding economic development and Latina/o theater. On one hand, the group emphasized the urgent need to develop data about Latina/o not-for-profit arts organizations, especially their revenue streams (grants, donations, earned cash). Several group members expressed concern that a generation of Latina/o professionals who might have donated to arts organizations has been "lost," while others commented on a perceived resistance among Latina/o philanthropists regarding sustaining donations to arts organizations. On the other hand, members of the group wondered whether that conventional development model is best suited to our audiences and our work, and whether enough attention has been given to gathering data about small-donation campaigns.

Before the larger assembly, Kevin Becerra summarized each of these statements of principles briefly. " … We need as a group to define and address the systemic issues in the infrastructure of producing, the climate of philanthropy, and the institutional funders." Becerra affirmed the group's conviction that "We need to find power in collaboration in our community, both locally and internationally…. [And] we need to assess where we are in relation to where we were in 1986. …When we meet in thirty years, what will we say?" Becerra then spoke about the group's interest in "upping the quality of Latina/o work" as a means of enhancing Latina/o artistic visibility. He shared the group's proposal that we find "a supported amount of money that can allow small companies to join organizations like TCG, to help defray the costs of memberships."

As the group prepared to leave the stage, Mario Ernesto Sánchez stepped forward to lead a shared breathing exercise. Sanchez invited the group to join him in proclaiming "Cuba!"

"We need to assess where we are in relation to where we were in 1986. …When we meet in thirty years, what will we say?" —Kevin Becerra

Conocimiento Group 7

The seventh and final *conocimiento* group gathered those affiliated primarily with ensembles. This group included Juan Amador (DJ Wonway), Nancy García Loza, Richard Montoya, Jesus Reyes, Chantal Rodriguez, Luis Valdez, Lupe Valdez, Mark Valdez, and Abigail Vega.

The ensemble *conocimiento's* conversation began with introductions, with each speaker offering a brief biography emphasizing how youthful encounters with theater practice—in preschool, grade school, college, early adulthood—instigated a lifelong journey. Early on, the conversation addressed the question of how ensemble theatermaking is both Latina/o theater's past and, more emphatically, its future. Contributors discussed how ensemble work permits one to enter the practice of theatermaking from the bottom; how it builds an art practice through the hard, complicated work of relationship-building with both collaborators and an audience; and how it rehearses techniques of improvisation, collaboration, participation, and inclusion, all in service to the task of bringing theater to its audience. At the same time, the group acknowledged the ways that, despite the legacy and success of ensembles like El Teatro Campesino and Culture Clash, the United States economy persists in valuing—in terms of both compensation and recognition—the individual artist. This individualist orientation contributes to problems of longevity for ensembles, whose members (who often wear an assortment of organizational hats) are often compelled to depart the ensemble in order to seek the sorts of individual opportunities that promise more adequate compensation.

Later in the day, the conversation emphasized two main threads: first, the group explored the question of Latina/o identity and its implications on both cultural and economic registers. Some asked what it meant to emphasize Latina/o identity as a cultural and creative question, while others wondered about Latina/o identity as a way to open questions about the institutional and economic relationships arts organizations have with their audience. More than one contributor mentioned the paradox of "pay what you can" performances, which not infrequently yield more revenue than conventional ticket sales. Others asked about whether the complicated challenges of *Latinidad* can be an opportunity to bring Latinas/os together. Next, the group raised the question of collaboration and partnership among Latina/o companies. Contributors noted that Latina/o ensembles are often isolated by the pressure of real estate and their particular local challenges of audience and donor development, as well as the increased expectations of audiences for productions of higher technical quality (both in terms of actual technology and theatrical technique). The group asked how might Latina/o theater be a movement of purpose, rather than an accumulation of individual successes and contemplated the possible value of Latina/o ensembles coming together to form reciprocal relationships, partnerships and collaborations. Contributors noted that Latina/o ensembles presently form partnerships with mainstream or non-Latina/o companies, not other Latina/o companies and observed that the isolation of Latina/o companies from one another diminished Latina/o theater's potential to grow as a movement ("We're not at the end of the movement; we're still at its beginning").

In their group presentation, Richard Montoya called to those assembled, "Everybody say hey oh!" The audience responded, and Montoya continued in call-and-response, he beginning each line, the audience responding by repeating his words and phrases.

> How might Latina/o theater be a movement of purpose, rather than an accumulation of individual successes?

RICHARD MONTOYA:	CROWD:
Hey oh…	Hey oh!
Teatro…	*Teatro*!
Ensemble…	Ensemble!
Say orange…	Orange!
Kashi…	Kashi!
Brezel…	*Brezel!*
Luis Valdez…	Luis Valdez!

LUIS VALDEZ:	CROWD:
Sí se puede…	*Sí se puede!*
Sí se puede…	*Sí se puede!*
Sí se puede…	*Sí se puede!*
Beatbox Juan Amador!	

Juan Amador then took the mic and announced "Theme one!" and began beatboxing, which underscored the next rounds of recitations first by Chantal Rodriguez, then by Abigail Vega, and finally by both together. Rodriguez and Vega spoke words derived from the *conocimiento's* discussions. *[Amador's beatbox continues throughout]*

CHANTAL RODRIGUEZ:
Identity
Expand the definition of *Latinidad*
Inclusivity
Intersectionality
Latinos are becoming more American
Anglos are becoming more Latino

JUAN AMADOR:

Theme two! Theme Two!

ABIGAIL VEGA:

Audience development

Serve the needs of the audience

Doing plays that matter

Sustainability

Engaging the audience where they are

Doing plays that matter

JUAN AMADOR:

Theme three! Theme three! Theme three!

RICHARD MONTOYA:	**CROWD:**
Say hey oh…	Hey oh!
HowlRound…	HowlRound!
Se puede…	*Se puede!*

CHANTAL RODRIGUEZ:

Economics

ABIGAIL VEGA:

Access

CHANTAL RODRIGUEZ:

Relationship to funders

ABIGAIL VEGA:

Need to create and develop new models

RICHARD MONTOYA:

Se puede, se puede, se puede

JUAN AMADOR:

All right we break it down like this
Discussing everything it's telling me
First of all we have identity
Everything we do we understand what we are usually
We must break it down and have a new time of inclusivity
Intersectionality
Everything that we've created
Everything we are can't be boxed into the normal type of action
We have to break it down what it is to be Latino and expand it
On a different level understand it's really about the audience
We really need to cultivate and build a whole new audience
That comes from building communities and rappers
Connecting all the players and making some plays that matter
And people are connected every time we try to rap this
But unfortunately we have to deal with all the economies
And all that stuff
Usually it's kind of whack
So many dope *teatros* but so little access
Let's guarantee what we do and keep it clean
Thank you so much, team seven, and these are our three themes.

"*Sí Se Puede*," the group chanted, as they returned to their seats. *[Huge applause]*

Friday Closing

"For real, that's a rap that I would buy. And write the check tomorrow," said Clyde Valentín. He invited the group to shout out the words that resonated as guiding thematics across the *conocimiento* group presentations.

> *Hope!*
> *Orgullo!*
> *Leadership!*
> *Dedication!*
> *Legacy!*
> *Esperanza!*
> *Economics!*
> *Ownership!*
> *Power!*
> *Hunger!*
> *Responsibility for the future!*
> *Cariño!*

"Tomorrow we're going to need some *cariño*," Valentín observed, as he encouraged to the group to "take this energy and bottle it up and preserve it for tomorrow as we go into the big day!" Olga Sanchez then invited the group to reflect on the day being "the first day of *día de los muertos, día de los anjelitos*, or the day that celebrates *los niños*." She continued:

> *A funny thing happened on the way to the Convening. A press re-*
> *lease was created and translated and sent out across the country to*
> *announce this event. It reached Boston City Hall. Boston City Hall*

*said, "Wow! That's really curious. We'd like to honor that in some
way. Can you write something up?" And so Tlaloc and a few other
folks [wrote] a document that will now be read by Sandra Delgado.*

SANDRA DELGADO:
It's official!

*[Holds a single folder bearing the Boston city seal. Reads the full
text of the mayor's proclamation followed by huge ovation, with
a first wave of applause gliding toward a rousing, rhythmic cheer,
punctuated by handclaps]*

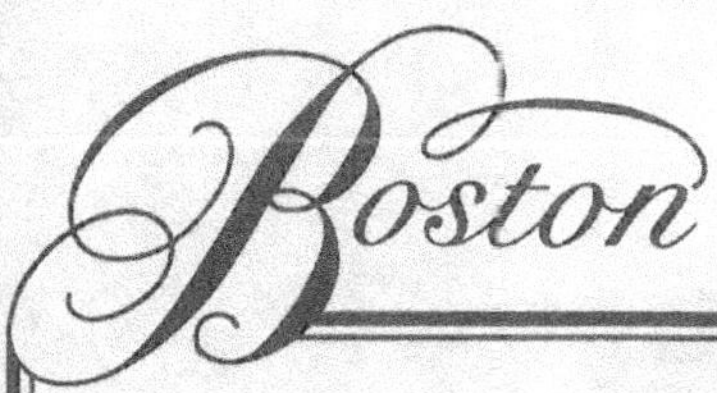

PROCLAMATION

Whereas: The Latina/o community is growing rapidly and creating positive impact in Boston and around the nation; and Latina/o Theatre is a prism through which communities view the multicultural qualities that support understanding & unity among all peoples; and

Whereas: The Latina/o Theatre Commons, founded in 2012, is a new platform for Latina/o theatre artists and advocates to support and nurture the stories of Latina/os on U.S. stages; and is already recognized as a vital force in American theatre; and endeavors to fulfill its promise to reshape the narrative of Latina/os in the U.S.; and

Whereas: The Latina/o Theatre Commons chose the city of Boston as the site for its first national gathering; inspired by Boston's history as a city of change and innovation and supported by the hospitality of HowlRound: A Center for the Theater Commons at Emerson College and the Doris Duke Charitable Foundation; and

Whereas: Latina/o theatre artists have a centuries-long history of contributing major works to world theater; and 21st century Latina/o theatre artists are carrying on that tradition; NOW

Therefore, I, Thomas M. Menino, Mayor of the City of Boston, do hereby proclaim Friday, November 1, 2013 to be

Latina/o Theatre Day

in the City of Boston.

Thomas M. Menino
____
Mayor

X-7130

FIG. 13

99

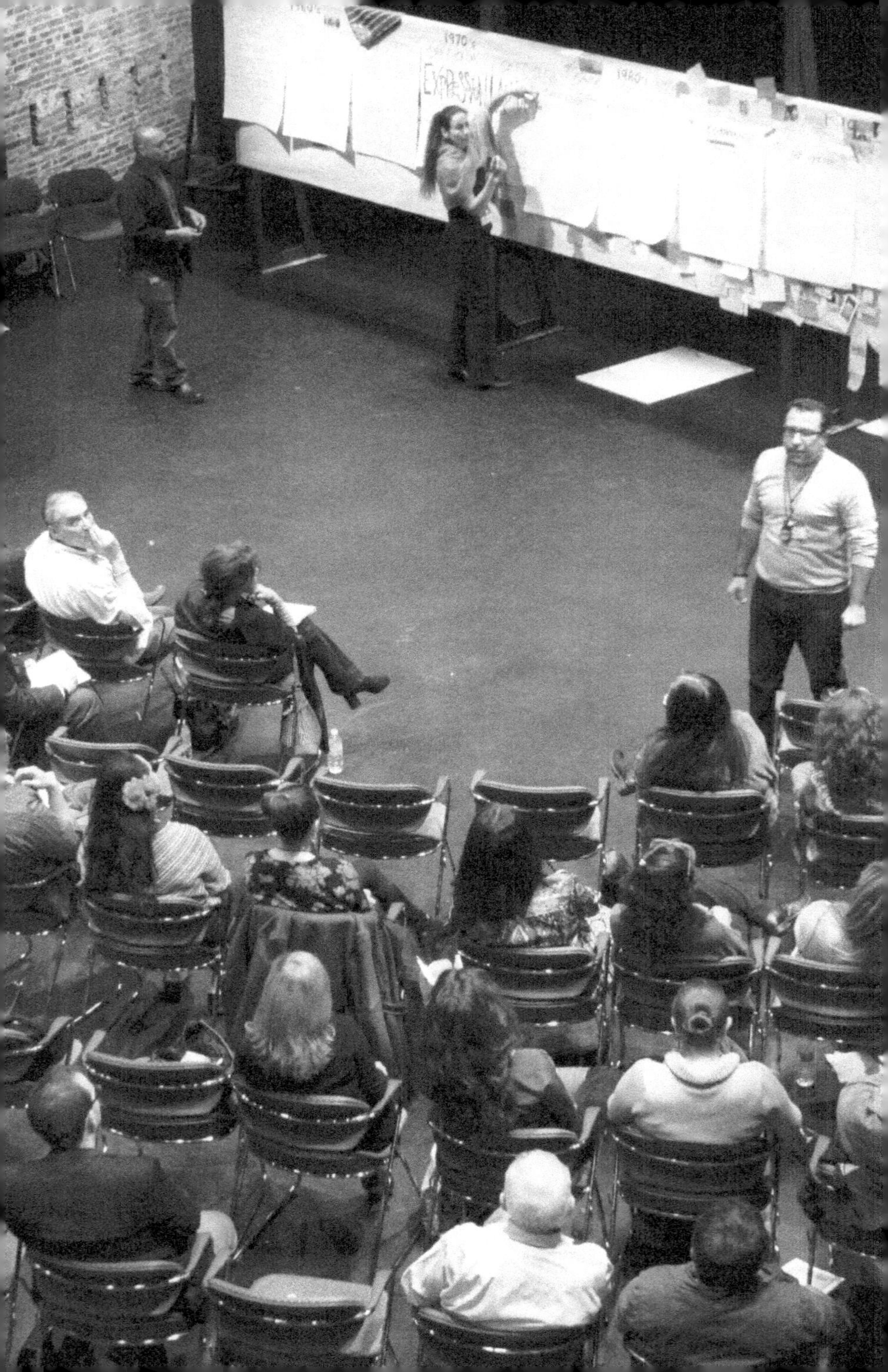

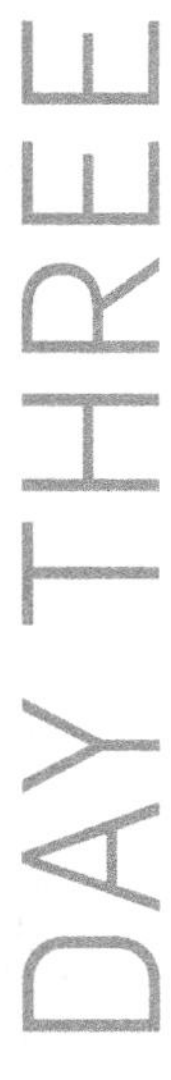

DAY THREE

Saturday 2 November

The Convening's third and final day was dedicated to assessing how the participants might pool the wisdom they carried, so as to share it with the broader network of Latina/o theatermakers. The morning's first session was dedicated to a plenary conversation about various national models of leadership, collaboration, communication, and co-presentation in place throughout the country. This plenary conversation was followed by *conocimiento* conversations among small "wisdom" groups organized according to participants' number of years in the field. Next, the Convening's circle widened for a historic session, "Voices from the Regions," in which small groups of Latina/o theatermakers from five cities (Chicago, Dallas, Los Angeles, Miami, and New York) joined the conversation in Boston via Skype live. Then, drawing upon the insights shared throughout the gathering, the group in Boston again broke out into smaller groups for a series of strategy conversations, this time according to their proposed contributions to the future work of the LTC. Thus over the course of the Convening, each participant was part of three distinct *conocimiento* groups based on: affiliation, years of experience, and strategy.

The day's work concluded with reports from each of the eight strategy *conocimientos* (Scholarship, Art-Making, Café Onda, Festivals, Advocacy, Convenings, Mentorship, and Networking), which were then distilled by the full group into four areas of strategic engagement for the LTC as it moved forward. The Convening's final day also included an unscheduled exercise dedicated to manifesting a "mentorship tree" among Convening participants, as well as a closing ceremony to bring the Convening to its full circle.

Co-facilitator Clyde Valentín invited those gathered to share any epiphanies they may have experienced as a result of the previous day's activities. Josefina López, playwright and artistic director of Los Angeles's Casa 0101, observed that "producing theater is so much easier if we ride on the wings of other people" as she reflected on the importance of sharing resources. Director José Carrasquillo marveled at the ways the convening permitted a clarity of vision about "where we are and where we are going" as Latina/o theatermakers. Playwright and director Amparo Garcia-Crow reflected on "how gorgeous it is to surrender to something bigger," noting "the awareness that I have of you in here is that we are passing the baton, but running at the same time." Then, playwright and director Luis Valdez ruminated on his own career as proof that "time goes by very quickly." He noted that theater is "a continuum," and elaborated upon Garcia-Crow's metaphor, "We are all passing the baton, and we belong to this long river in the theater."

Valentín mirrored the insight that the work of the Convening was itself a "dynamic, moving force.[...] We know there is a lot to come."

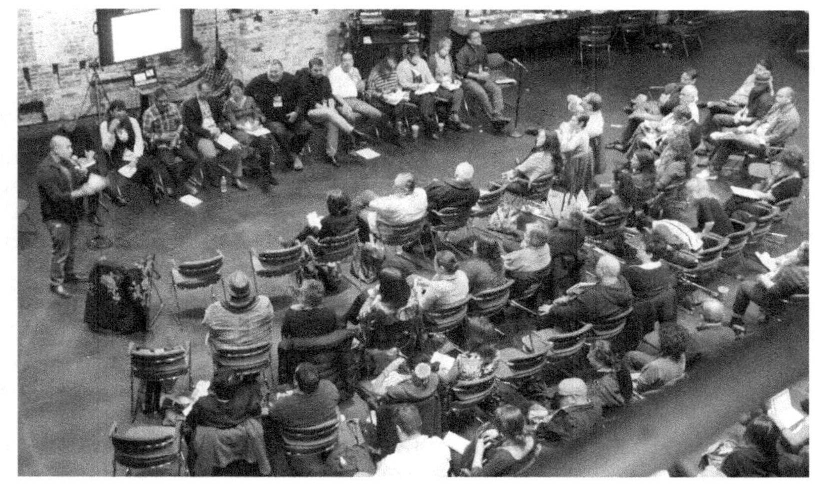

FIG. 15

PLENARY PANEL: Expanding Our Environmental Analysis

The morning's plenary session, "Expanding Our Environmental Analysis," sought to develop and share a bird's-eye view of the national trends, initiatives, and organizations of potential relevance to the work of Latina/o theatermakers. The panel invited speakers in four flights, each addressing a particular national (and not necessarily Latina/o-specific) model of engagement: Leadership, Collaboration, Communication, and Co-Presentation (for example, festivals). Each invited speaker addressed the audience for a handful of minutes to introduce the organization and reflect on the relevance of its model to the larger group.

LEADERSHIP

Abel López spoke of Americans for the Arts as an organization dedicated to building informed arts leaders for whom diversity was not an initiative but a core programmatic principle. Diane Rodriguez discussed the role of Theater Communications Group (TCG) as a service organization for theatermakers. She underscored the organization's strategic commitments to diversification of theater boards, audiences, and production

103

models. Mark Valdez spoke of the Network of Ensemble Theaters and its commitment to the principle that "if you build community, you build capacity." Next, scholars Noe Montez and Patricia Ybarra respectively detailed the missions of the American Society for Theater Research (ASTR) and the Association for Theatre in Higher Education (ATHE), each emphasizing the potential for artists to be part of the scholarly conversation.

COLLABORATION

Chris Acebo described the Latina/o Play Project at the Oregon Shakespeare Festival and its commitment to incubating and presenting world premieres of new Latina/o plays. Kevin Becerra detailed the impact of the National New Play Network's "Rolling World Premiere," as well as the organization's launch of the New Play Exchange, an online platform dedicated to the secure, digital circulation of new play manuscripts among literary managers, artistic directors, and other theater professionals. Tony Garcia spoke of the National Performance Network's various projects dedicated to cultivating collaborative relationships among arts organizations.

COMMUNICATION

Caridad Svich was the first to discuss models of technology-driven communication. She described NoPassport, an unincorporated theater alliance and press that, through its seven consecutive conferences and a host of digital initiatives, seeks to cultivate a global community of theatermakers. Next, Irma Mayorga spoke of the digital networks (listserve, website) created by the Latina/o Focus Group of the Association for Theater in Higher Education as resources to all. Teresa Marrero detailed the operations of TCG 2.0, a digital initiative of the Theater Communications Group which through its website seeks to develop multiple streams of conversation about the American theater. Tlaloc Rivas then described Café Onda at HowlRound, the online arm of the LTC, which aims to become an online community dedicated to Latina/o theater in the United States. "The dream," Rivas concluded, "is to make [Café Onda] a home page for all of us."

At this juncture, co-facilitator Kinan Valdez guided a spontaneous "roll call," inviting those assembled to stand if they had accessed the resources of these ten organizations. "If you have written for Café Onda, please stand," Valdez prompted. As Valdez called through the list, typically a dozen or so of those gathered stood. After completing the roll call with the admonition that "all of us must access these resources," Clyde Valentín took over to moderate the plenary's next flight of discussion, regarding varied models of co-presentation and festivals.

Valentín spoke first about the particular potential of festivals as "a moment of now," a "means of coalescing and bringing people together in a particular way," affirming the potency of the performance festival as a mode of community organizing. Valentín then turned the focus to those panelists assembled and asked each to speak to how their particular festivals were organized.

Sandra Delgado spoke first about Yo Solo, a Chicago festival dedicated to Latina/o artists writing and performing their own work. Next, Diane Rodriguez spoke of co-founding RadarLA, an annual performance festival dedicated to ensemble works of

> "The dream is to make Café Onda a home page for all of us."
> —Tlaloc Rivas

collective creation emerging from Latin America, the Pacific Rim, and the western United States. Mario Ernesto Sánchez detailed the genesis and twenty-nine years of success of Miami's International Hispanic Theater Festival and its dedication to "preserving our Hispanic-Latino cultural heritage" through its presentation of the works of Hispanic-origin playwrights throughout Latin America and Spain. Mark Valdez described the community-based "microfests," produced by the Network of Ensemble Theaters, which aim to identify "under the radar" work happening in such locales as Appalachia, Detroit, Hawaii, and New Orleans. Finally, José Luis Valenzuela detailed the vision of collaborative exchange guiding the LTC 2014 Encuentro, and Lisa Portes sketched the "carnaval" idea at the heart of the LTC 2105 gathering in Chicago. The conversation then turned to a brief discussion of the challenges of programming, funding, marketing, and budgeting for (not infrequently multilingual) festivals. Valentín brought the session to a close.

Big Ideas from the Wisdom Groups

Facilitator Kinan Valdez prompted those assembled to find their next *conocimiento* groups and reminded everyone to catalog the many models of leadership, collaboration, communication, and co-presentation that might not yet be part of the Convening's conversation. "Bring those resources into the record," Valdez prompted, "give voice to those theatermakers who are not present." The eight *conocimiento* groups were framed as "Wisdom Groups" and organized according to the participant's self-reported years "in the field" of Latina/o theatermaking. (The configuration of these groups, as well as a listing of their contributors, can be referenced in the participant appendix to this volume.) With roughly ten contributors assigned to each group, the Wisdom Groups gathered throughout the Liebergott Black Box and its large outer lobby. Each Wisdom Group's moderator was charged with guiding the group participants through three general areas of conversation: to use their collective knowledge to list those festivals, institutions, and initiatives not named in the plenary; to consider models of leadership and communication; and finally, to dream toward the future. Each group typically began with brainstorming lists of those institutions, festivals, and initiatives that, in both the past and present, had demonstrated an emphatic commitment or openness to Latina/o theater artists and their work. Following the discussion of institutions and festivals, the Wisdom Groups moved beyond the brainstorming mode as they developed particular points of vision or critique on the questions of leadership, communication, and innovation.

Because it was assumed that the members of the Wisdom Groups would carry these ideas forward to their Strategy Sessions later in the day, there was no structured opportunity in the Convening's schedule to report on the Wisdom Group conversations to the broader group. To capture some of the work done in these sessions, the particular resources—organizations, initiatives, festivals named by each group's brainstorming conversation—have been collated into a single list that appears as an appendix to this volume. A partial aggregation of the insights, inspirations, and interventions percolating across the eight Wisdom Group conversations appears below.

Every Wisdom Group affirmed the urgent need for a freely accessible online database of and for contemporary Latina/o theatermakers.

Different groups emphasized different aspects of such a platform. Several groups imagined this database serving as an online archive for both contemporary and historical Latina/o theater with potential links to resources supporting production and educational initiatives. Some groups discussed the ways digital communication platforms permitted geographically separated artists to join the process of production in new ways, while also providing new mechanisms for audience development. Other groups envisioned an artist-driven data-mapping project that might be used toward advocacy and fundraising objectives. Most visions of such a database imagined it to be an essential resource both for Latina/o theater professionals and for non-Latina/o theater professionals seeking to identify Latina/o collaborators. Without exception, every Wisdom Group craved a freely accessible, interactive, and searchable digital platform that might provide current and easily updated information about contemporary Latina/o theater professionals as well as current listings of productions, companies, and relevant opportunities for artist and community engagement.

The convening's notable inclusion of both scholars and practitioners prompted several groups to contemplate the gaps between artistic and educational leadership.

Several Wisdom Groups noted the potential to leverage academia to support and sustain Latina/o theater practice. Some groups emphasized the priority of documentation of Latina/o theater's legacy, noting the comparative lack of accessible material (narratives, histories, memoirs) about Latina/o theater artists, companies, and movements of the recent past. Other groups wondered whether academia might provide a possible site for new work development or artistic residencies. Several groups affirmed an awareness that particular universities, professors, libraries, and academic societies might prove essential allies not only in the archiving and teaching of Latina/o theater texts and practice, but also as potential collaborators in the production of contemporary Latina/o work. These groups sought to identify worthy academic partners at both the institutional and individual level, and connect all rising students of Latina/o performance to national networks of artists and scholars.

The most consistent concern expressed across the Wisdom Groups was the persistent lack of adequate financial resources to sustain the cultivation and health of Latina/o theater artists, companies and initiatives.

Many groups affirmed the priority of developing innovative and sustained models of creative and professional mentorship, and several specifically invoked the legacy of María Irene Fornés in doing so. One group proposed "The Fornés Institute"—a mobile workshop anchored by a permanent space housing a library and artist's apartment that might permit the students of María Irene Fornés to carry forward her legacy as an artist, teacher, and mentor. Several groups affirmed both the need for and value of meaningful talent development programs for early- and mid-career artists (especially directors), noting the limited access to long-term mentorship models (artistic residencies, structured relationships with "master" artists) that cultivated relationships beyond the scope of a single production. Many groups wondered whether and where the leaders in Latina/o theater were being nurtured, noting the necessity of mentorship for "the art and science" of administration and advocacy. Some groups imagined supportive mentorship models addressing specific skills (grant writing, for example) while others reflected on the challenge of balancing one's individual aspirations as a maturing artist with the pressures of the profession, including one's service as administrator or educator; the difficulties of one's legibility within a changing world; and competition and power struggles among one's peers. Most groups expressed a hunger for greater access to relevant mentorship in areas of arts leadership and a desire to connect the wisdom of previous eras to the particular challenges of the contemporary moment.

Perhaps the most consistent concern expressed across the Wisdom Groups was the persistent lack of adequate financial resources to sustain the cultivation and health of Latina/o theater artists, companies, and initiatives. Several groups expressed concern about debilitating problems posed by the persistently limited financial resources of Latina/o theater companies and how that lack of money suppressed the growth of the field in resource intensive areas, including marketing, outreach, audience development, and appropriate compensation for artists.

Voices from the Regions

"The entire country is on this call!" —Olga Sanchez

Immediately upon the resolution of the conversations of the Wisdom Groups, the full convening reassembled in the Liebergott Black Box to participate in an ambitious experiment to bring "voices from the regions" into the Boston Convening conversation.

Using Skype video conferencing in tandem with livestreaming

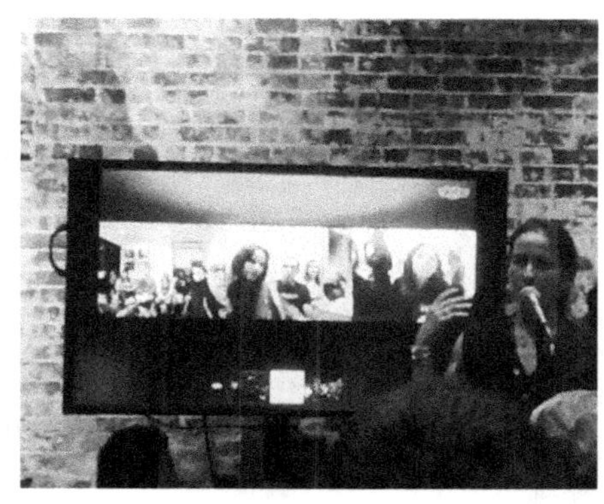

through HowlRound TV, HowlRound orchestrated a group conversation involving Latina/o theatermakers from cities across the country. Facilitator Olga Sanchez welcomed each of the regional teams and invited each group to introduce itself.

In Miami, Joann María Yarrow, Artistic Director of Miami's Teatro Prometeo, and actor Jorge Hernandez led the conversation. In New York, playwright Beto O'Byrne spoke on behalf of nearly twenty assembled artists, with support from playwrights Christina Quintana and Carmen Rivera Tirado, as well as Prégones Theater's Rosalba Rolon. In Chicago, about twenty Latina/o theatermakers gathered, with Sindy Castro, Elizabeth Nungaray, and Isaac Gomez guiding the conversation. In Los Angeles, Armando Huipe and Fanny Garcia moderated a conversation that included a diverse group of about a dozen contributors. In Dallas, scholar/educator Lorenzo Garcia along with Frida Lozano, artistic associate with Cara Mía theater, led the conversation among the members of TANTO, or the *Teatro Alianza* of North Texas Organizations.

As each group spoke, a video image (when available) was projected on a screen in the Liebergott. These five windows served as a virtual portal bringing these additional voices (more than fifty in total) into the Convening's conversation. Over the next hour, the groups took turns addressing

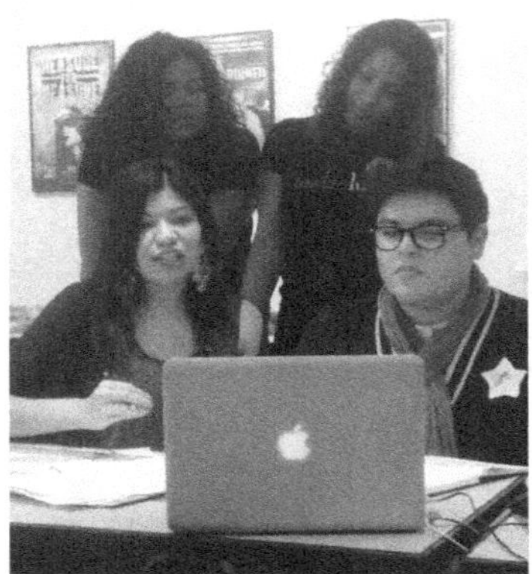

The experiment bringing the "Voices from the Regions" into the convening proved to be a powerful gesture animating the premise guiding the convening.

two principle questions: How do you describe your Latina/o theatermaking community? How does your community work together to address the shared concerns of the goals and visions of your Latina/o theatermakers?

The groups spoke in turn, moving in a rotation that carried the conversation from the southeast to the northeast, across the midwest, to the west, and then to the southwest. As they described what made their particular communities distinct, several unifying themes emerged: first, the importance of artistic self-determination; second, interest in sharing resources in a way that might build their Latina/o theatermaking community; third, the challenges of accessing current information about all the Latina/o theatermaking happening in their communities; and fourth, a desire to participate in a national flow of ideas, information, and collaboration. The groups also affirmed their various strategies for exploring cross-cultural collaborations, while honoring the culturally-specific heritages and traditions of activism that brought their theaters into being. Throughout, the groups expressed enthusiasm about the prospect of resource and skill-sharing and hopes for a greater sense of collaboration and solidarity among Latina/o theatermakers.

The technological capacity that made this conversation possible also contributed its share of technical challenges. The spirit of conversational exchange and dialogue that had guided the convening was challenged by routine mishaps of any conference call (speakers not knowing whether they were being heard, disparate levels of audio/video quality), all of which was complicated by the struggle to maintain a spirit of openness and sharing within a snug window of time allotted to this session. Additionally, the "howlround" (or the sonic effect created when the sounds from a loudspeaker feed back into the microphone) amplified the uncertainty among speakers as to whether they should speak or could be heard. (Ironically, the "howlround effect" also created an instructional moment, when all those gathered— including facilitator Sanchez—learned the meaning behind the name of the organization hosting the Convening.)

Yet, for all its limitations and technical challenges, the experiment bringing the "Voices from the Regions" into the convening proved to be a powerful gesture animating the premise guiding the Convening. Fittingly enough, the #CaféOnda twitter feed erupted with responses to the experiment. Some commented on the palpable excitement infusing the experiment.

@howlround: The energy here is electric.

@JosefinaLopez: So exciting to have theater artists from Miami, NYC, LA, Chicago and Dallas with us… to add to the conversation and dreams.

Others commented on the emotion stirred by the experience.

@teatroluna: Words cannot articulate the beauty of this

@pollykcarl: Listening to all of these cities join the conversation very emotional for the entire room

@CXA: Ok. This is making me weep.

Twitter also brought voices from beyond the Liebergott commenting on the experience of this experiment.

@CARTheater: Now that's what I call a national dialogue. I feel blessed just to witness this.

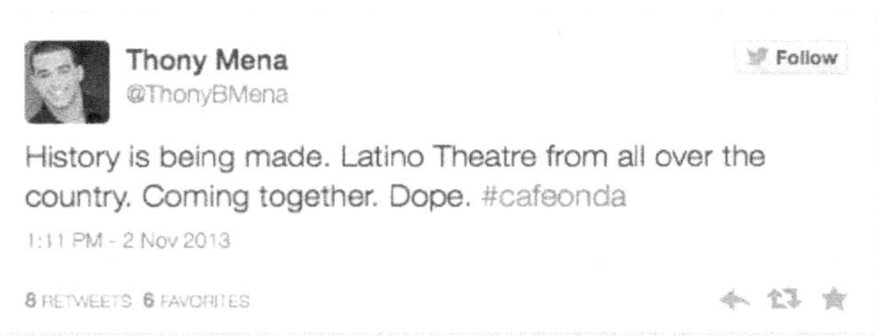

FIG. 18

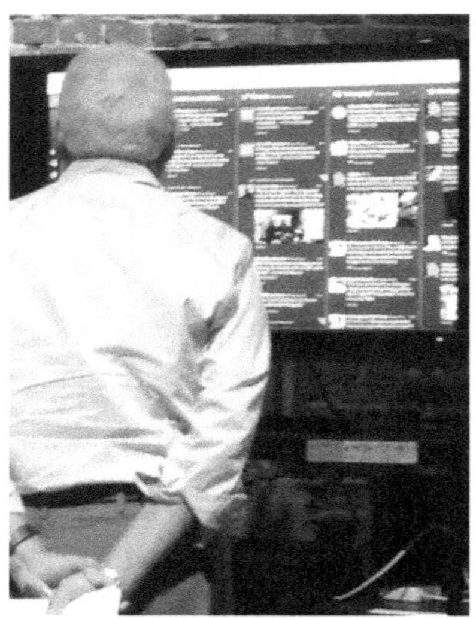

The session concluded as those assembled in Boston stood to recognize their peers from around the country and reassert the sense of national solidarity guiding the premise and purpose of the Convening itself.

FIG. 19

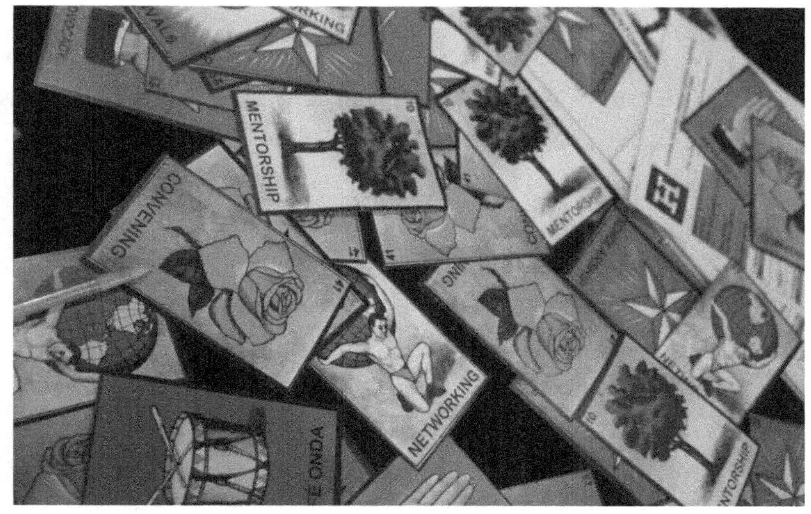

Choosing Strategic Directions

Immediately after the "Voices from the Regions" session, those in Boston were invited to reassemble in "Strategy Groups," according to their *lotería* card assignment.

Upon their arrival to the Convening two days prior, attendees had been given a card assigning them to one of eight strategy groups. Each card displayed a colorful image derived from *lotería*, the traditional Mexican game of chance. On each card, the name of a strategy group appeared where the card's title would typically appear: advocacy (*la mano*), art-making (*el musico*), Café Onda (*el tambor*), convenings (*la rosa*), festivals (*el sol*), mentoring (*el arbol*), networking (*el mundo*), and scholarship (*la estrella*). Though each participant had been assigned a card upon arrival, the Convening's co-facilitators had exhorted participants throughout the proceedings to swap cards if they wished to join a different strategy conversation. As the full group began to sort itself into its new Strategy groups, and as this swapping continued, the facilitators reminded each group of its task in the Strategy Sessions: to draw upon the wisdom gathered in all the listening sessions and small group conversations as they crafted a single-sentence strategic vision statement. One hour later, the groups gathered to present their particular recommendations for the full group's consideration.

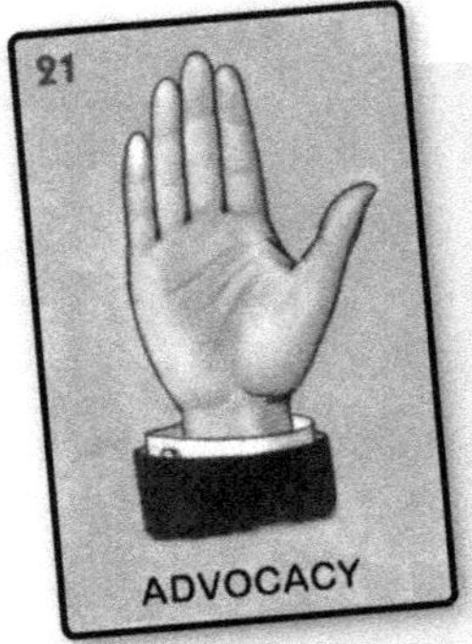

EL MANO

The Advocacy group engaged in a far-reaching conversation about the structural and financial challenges to establishing equity of access, representation, and commitment to Latina/o artists and their communities. The group's summary report called for the cultivation of "a strong community of advocates" that would include artists, administrators, and audiences well-trained and adept at integrating advocacy into all aspects of making Latina/o theater. The group concluded with a call to build reciprocal relationships between local advocacy initiatives and larger, national organizations.

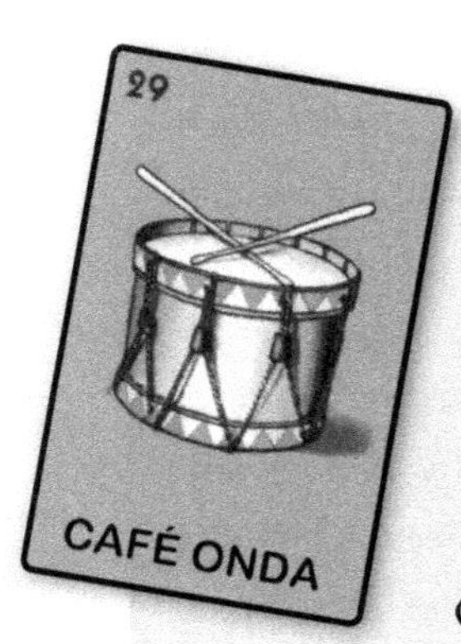

EL TAMBOR

The Café Onda group's freewheeling and energetic conversation focused on the need for the LTC to create an independent website that would serve as a dynamic, interactive digital hub for everything to do with Latina/o theater and those making it. The group imagined Café Onda's extensive functionality, including an interactive database of Latina/o theaters and theatermakers; a freely accessible archive of contemporary and historical Latina/o theater; and hosting capacity for production support materials (or dramaturgical protocols) for new Latina/o plays. In summary, the group offered three keywords: expression, advocacy, and networking as the primary vectors of content and engagement for Café Onda.

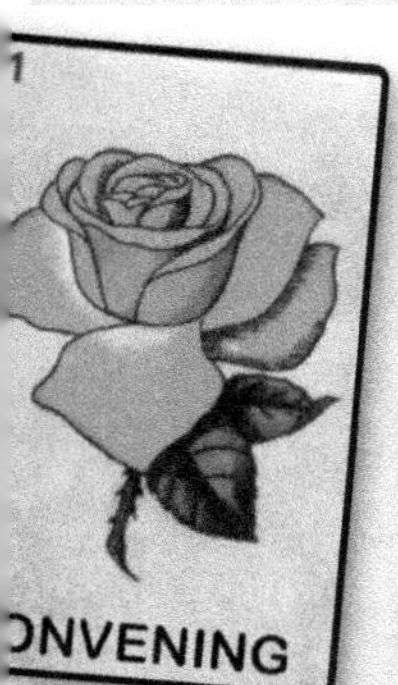

LA ROSA

The Convening group began by adventurously envisioning what a Latina/o Theater Convening might look like in 2046. The themes of intergenerational and intercultural exchange that informed the group's vision also guided the statement they presented in summary: "We envision in 2046 a shift from 'us' in our Convening to a 'we' as our racial diversity and hybridity becomes realized. We envision multigenerational Convenings with blurred geographical (and perhaps metaphysical) borders, attended by thousands and blessed by a Latina president." Strategies for this vision include the need to organize locally, regionally, and nationally; to draw upon existing community-based models; to rotate the location of future Convenings; and to commit "to really do this."

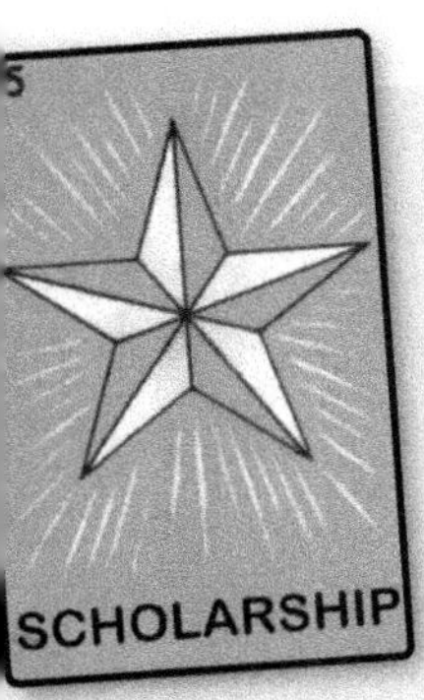

LA ESTRELLA

The Scholarship group affirmed that artists and scholars shared the responsibility for documentation of Latina/o theater making. The group agreed that, in spite of its limitations, academia's resources might be leveraged more effectively in service of Latina/o theatermakers. In summary, the group offered two main strategies, collaboration and documentation, to cultivate academia as a hospitable site for both the collaborative development of contemporary Latina/o theater, and the archival documentation of its legacy.

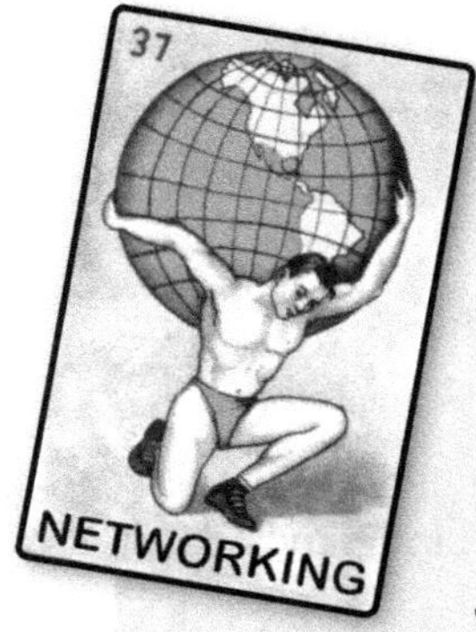

EL MUNDO

The Networking group sought to fortify greater connections among the many existing networks of Latina/o theater professions and affirmed that networking among Latina/o artists was a form of strategic collaboration. Identifying key obstacles (geography, digital literacy, personality), the group seized upon mentorship—opening doors for one another so as to fortify access to access—as its guiding theme. In summary, the group called upon everyone "to expand, support, and illuminate Latinas/os in the American theater field" through deliberate participation in existing programs, careful integration of regional partners, and strategic use of digital resources (like Café Onda).

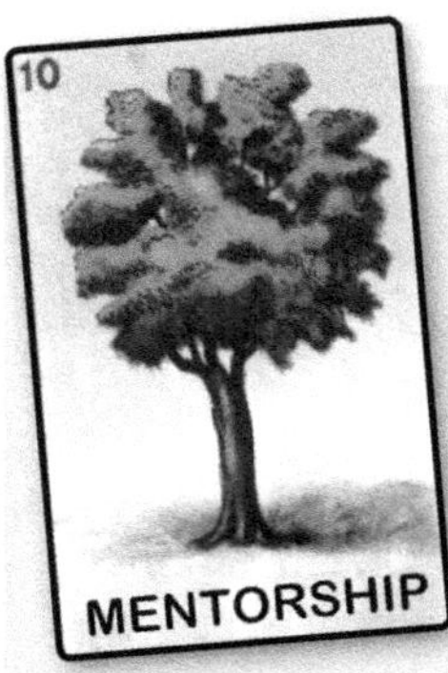

EL ARBOL

The Mentorship group engaged in a searching conversation about the meaning of mentorship, both in principle and in practice, as the participants reflected upon "best practices" of mentorship as well as innovative techniques (and technologies) applicable to the work of mentorship. In summary, the group affirmed that arts leaders at every phase of their careers needed (and deserved) mentors, and that every arts leader must think of herself or himself as both a mentor and one deserving of mentorship. The group called for the cultivation of mentorship—of holding the door open so that others might enter—as a defining principle of Latina/o theater practice.

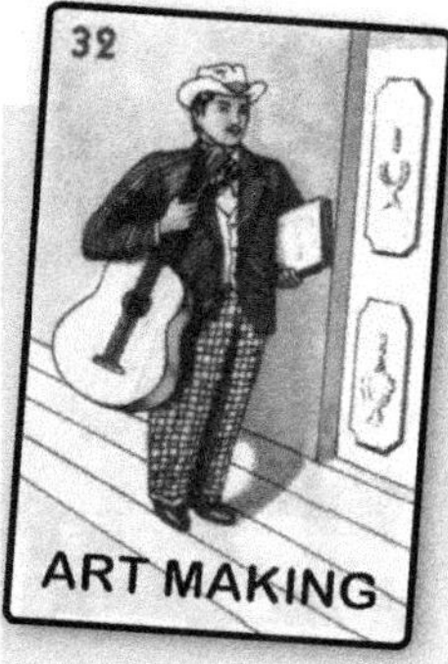

EL MUSICO

The Art-Making group asserted that creativity must be valued as a precious, abundant resource within Latina/o communities. The group affirmed that the empathy for human experience and understanding that lives in every individual artist would create an artistic community without borders. In summary, the group imagined a future in which artists would be valued members of society, in which stories would reflect the community, in which institutions and collaborations would engage all disciplines and regions, and in which an inclusive "multiorgasmic" dramatic structure would evolve to encompass women's stories in a world where love and respect greets the making of art.

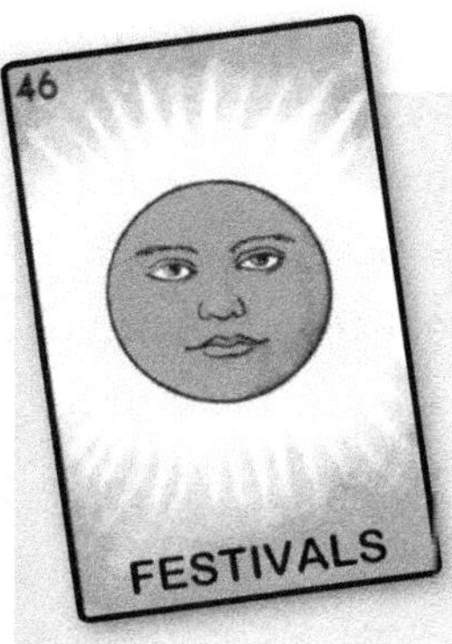

EL SOL

The Festivals group dedicated their conversation to envisioning two events on the horizon for the LTC community: the 2014 *Encuentro* in Los Angeles and the 2015 *Carnaval* in Chicago. With the *Encuentro* guided by the premise of companies of artists coming together in the spirit of

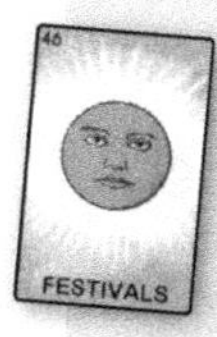

rigorous exchange, and the *Carnaval* imagined as a concentrated week highlighting particular works and techniques, the conversation emphasized the challenges and opportunities promised by both events. In summary, the group affirmed that "direct and respectful artistic encounters" would both "celebrate and reveal artistic excellence" while fortifying creative and professional connections among a national community of Latina/o artists.

Four main strategy

areas were

identified:

Advocacy;

Art-Making;

Convening/

Networking; and

Scholarship.

Upon conclusion of each strategy group's summary report, and with the large sheets of paper summarizing each group's recommendations blanketing the Latina/o theater timeline, Kinan Valdez stepped forward "to weave the narratives, the visions, that have been created" with a poem "quilted" from the words just spoken by the conveners.

Valdez's poetic summary of the work of the strategy groups elicited a rousing round of applause. His co-facilitators then invited those assembled to think toward distilling all the ideas offered into three or four specific strategy directives for the LTC to take forward in its work beyond the Convening. The task was "not to edit, but to build" a vision for the LTC, while also consolidating the many strategic recommendations toward those areas where the LTC might be able to effect the greatest impact. The co-facilitators pressed the group to evince what was layered within and across the recommendations throughout the Convening's many circles. With some participants calling out ideas and revisions, and others stepping to the microphones to offer more extended observations, the co-facilitators guided the group's process until four main strategy areas were identified: Advocacy; Art-Making; Convening /Networking; and Scholarship.

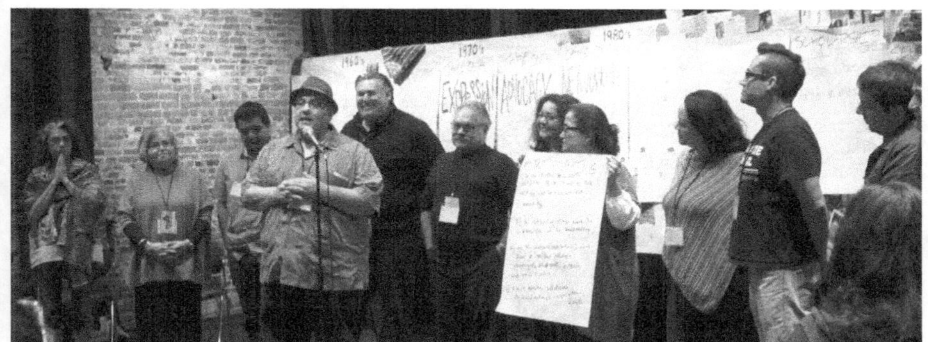

The process also affirmed that certain key recommendations (Café Onda, The Fornés Institute, and Mentorship) were central within all four of these strategy areas, and that certain priorities remained, including the need for digital access to information and resources and the necessity for "deliberate infiltration" by Latina/o theatermakers within existing national, regional, and local organizations. With the energy still high and the session barely resolved, the co-facilitators invited the participants to gather in the lobby just outside the Leibergott Black Box for an unscheduled event: "The Mentorship Tree."

Poem "quilted" by Kinan Valdez from the words spoken during each strategy group's summary report.

In the following, we wish not to do to others what has been done to us.

We envision in 2046 a shift from "us" in our convening to a "we" as our racial diversity and hybridity becomes realized.

We envision an effective understanding of advocacy and a strong group of advocates.

We envision Café Onda as an online hub for expression, advocacy, and networking for Latina/o theater.

We envision scholars in the theaters and artists in the universities.

We envision convenings that are multigenerational with blurred geographic and perhaps metaphysical borders, attended by thousands, and blessed by a Latina president.

We acknowledge as activists in the field that there is an abundance in networks and access and that we—through convening, mentorship, open platforms, and existing national programs—aim to expand, support, and illuminate Latinas/os in the American theater field.

We envision collaborative thinking and relationship building.

We envision cultivation of a mentorship culture.

We envision [that] direct and respectful artistic encounters over a four-week period at the LATC Encuentro will assess the level of artistic excellence of our field.

We envision eight pieces representing the four directions in a Carnaval of the theater.

In the theater of Inlakech in 2046, the artist will be the most valued member of the community, by reflecting stories where the communities can see themselves. The castles and institutions each will have a resident scholar, resident playwright, resident designer, and a group of actors, all working together to collaborate on local, national, and international levels.

And we envision love and respect existing with artists at the center creating multiorgasmic, spiraling theater in 2046!

The Mentorship Tree Exercise

One of the few unscheduled events in the Convening's tightly plotted schedule was the "Mentorship Tree" exercise, which took place in the brief space of time allotted for a break in an afternoon otherwise dedicated to strategy selection and next steps for LTC. The "Mentorship Tree" exercise was guided by Micha Espinosa and Marcos Nájera, in response to a suggestion by Tiffany Ana López.

Reflecting on the collective creation of both the altar and timeline as "collective archives" of both presence and witness, López took inspiration from the *arbol* image on the Mentorship *lotería* card. "What would it look like," López wondered, "to create an embodied mentoring tree that physically illustrated the connections of everyone in the room and their generational passing forward of history through the sharing of knowledge and training?" López offered the idea to co-facilitator Olga Sanchez, who enlisted voice specialist Micha Espinosa's expertise in integrating it into the next day's program.

Drawing from López's initial inspiration, Espinosa developed the Convening's "Mentorship Tree Exercise," a voice and movement experience designed "to map the past and facilitate future connections" among the theatermakers gathered at the Convening. Espinosa conceived of the exercise as one in which "we would map our own bodies for tensions and release tension" from a day full of "sitting, thinking, and listening," thereby "healing the mind/body split" that so easily comes after such work. "We began by relocating into the lobby," Espinosa recalled, "finding our space in the room, and gently moving our bodies, finding the spine, and then allowing our spines to dance." Espinosa and Nájera guided the participants to allow their breath "to drop in and flow out" and to use that shared breath (and eventually the hum of the group's voice) "as a collective to bring forth the truth that resonates within us."

Espinosa and Nájera then invited the group to reflect on their relationship to their mentors, to take the "hum into [their] hands and hearts" and guide their intention to the mentorship offered by Luis Valdez and María Irene Fornés.

"Micha charged us to explore our physical relationship to our past mentors, our mentees, our future mentor and mentees, all through movement," recalled playwright Elaine Romero. Espinosa and Nájera instructed participants to follow their breath and their bodies in an embodied meditation, listening to their bodily impulses for a psychological gesture expressing their "point of connection" with "an influence or inspiration." Tiffany Ana López described what followed as a "physical manifestation of the reverberating impact of mentoring."

Participants gathered, holding one another by the hand or the shoulder to manifest the sense of connection to and through one another. Luis Valdez stood toward one side of the space and, with María Irene Fornés too ill to attend the Convening, her student Migdalia Cruz was asked to stand as her surrogate. López noted how a "tree" of connections quickly spiraled around Luis Valdez, as he "touched Jorge Huerta with Diane Rodriguez, Olga Garay, and so many others… within the tableau." Romero recalled how "I found my hand grasping toward Migdalia as she blended into Irene," and Espinosa noted that Fornés' "energetic blueprint stemmed and branched out, emanating from a central point." As these connections were discovered, the energy in the space built. Recognizing what she called "a vortex of energy" surrounding Valdez (and acknowledging

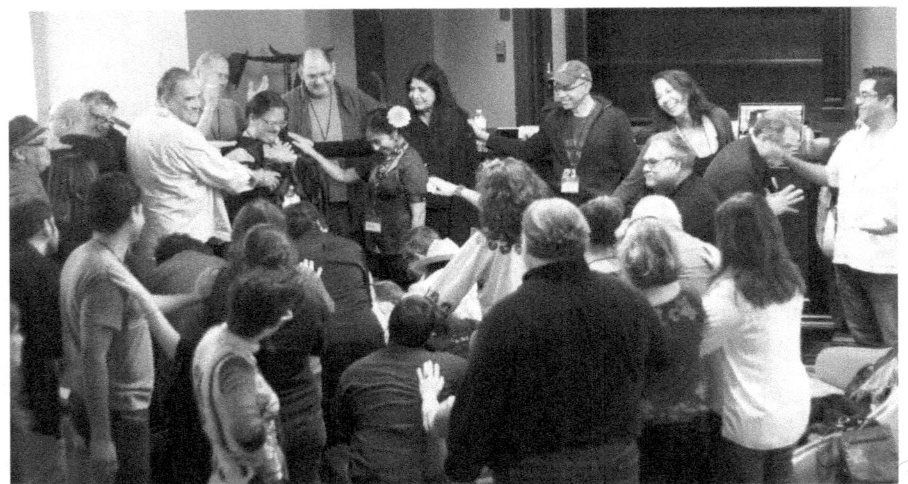

FIG. 22

the surge of collective emotion now held by Cruz), Espinosa then guided the participants to "move slowly" and to "allow the movement to naturally subside." Espinosa recalled, "We honored the connections and then began to move around the room again [with] the same state of readiness" as we "looked for new threads and stems we might create."

Romero recalled, "Micha asked us to find potential mentors. Lisa Portes walked up to me and said, 'We mentor each other.' I told Octavio Solis that he had mentored me." Soon, a new "tree" of mentorship formed, as López noted, in which "nearly all participants were moving together in an improvised dance that affirmed our historical connection and continuity." Of this moment, Romero recalled,

When, at last, our tree of mentorship was built, tears flowed. Our experiences of our mentors and each other transcended words, our years of experience needed this physical shape, a forest of experiences, an abrazo *from the collective whole, to be completely expressed.*

Espinosa and Nájera then guided the group to form three concentric circles "where we called upon our voices to chime together." For López, these circles, like "the concentric circles in which we sat for so much of the Convening," effected "another moment for contemplating our interconnectedness and experiencing the power of embodied storytelling and active listening/witnessing." Likewise, for Romero, "Micha's tree and our opening, encircled altar showed me that we, in the LTC, do not have a linear narrative or relationship between mentor and mentee, but a circular one." And, for Espinosa, the "Mentorship Tree" exercise created space for "being with each other, seeing each other, and sounding with each other; an atmosphere of curiosity, possibilities, and future interests emerged. We did not just imagine, but we physically manifested critical alliances to move our profession and our *cultura* forward."

Upon the resolution of the "Mentorship Tree" exercise, the group returned to the Leibergott Black Box for the final session of the Convening.

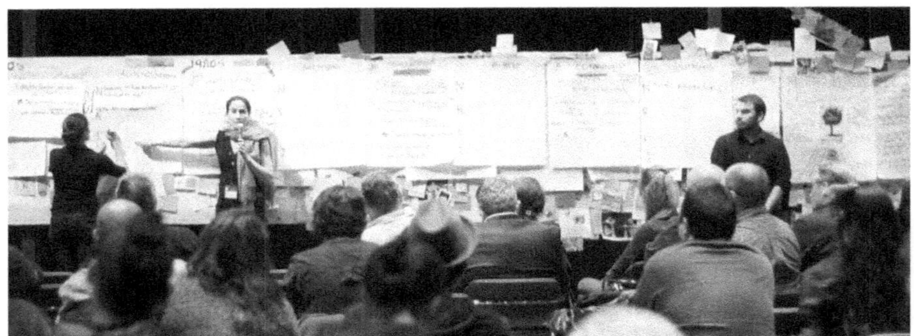

Strategy Selection

The group reassembled to craft strategy statements based on the conversations shared throughout the Convening. Co-facilitator Olga Sanchez guided the group's conversation. With the assistance of note-takers, participants articulated full strategic visions for each of the four areas: Advocacy; Art-Making; Convening/Networking; and Scholarship. For each statement of a strategic vision, the group was asked to identify national, regional, and local iterations of strategy. These statements of vision are listed below. Please note that the additional detail within the Advocacy summary reflects the greater amount of time dedicated to the discussion of its components; the later sections (Art-Making, Convening/Networking, and Scholarship) were composed more briskly.

ADVOCACY

The primary strategic direction is deliberate infiltration of existing networks via national, regional, local, and individual efforts.

On the national level, establish a dynamic, user-generated database of resources relevant to Latina/o theatermakers (perhaps along the lines of the National New Play Network) that includes:

- Professional profiles for artists: actors, designers, directors, dramaturgs, fundraisers, playwrights, producers, scholars, and technicians;

- A list of Latina/o theater leaders whose expertise might be of interest to foundations, boards, and policymakers; and

- A list of regional talent consultants for the reference of artistic directors, casting directors, and producers seeking Latina/o artists, producers, scholars, and/or technicians in a particular region.

Additional strategies on the national level include the development of a national advocacy plan guided by and connected to regional advocacy strategies:

- Leverage national consortiums, non-profits, unions, and other membership-based advocacy organizations toward transparency and accountability for their Latino/a members or constituents;

- Advocate for a "National Year of the Latina/o Play" to be undertaken by every theater in the country, asserting the priority of full productions on a regular basis; and

- Investigate the potential "rebranding" of the LTC as the "New Americans Theater Commons." Wouldn't we spell it the "American" way if rebranded?

On the regional and local level, develop an advocacy plan that is guided by and connects with national strategies:

- Hold local leaders (civic and philanthropic) accountable for their support of Latina/o arts organizations in the regions;

- Identify expert regional talent consultants to address hiring inquiries by artistic directors, casting directors, and producers seeking Latina/o theater professionals; and

- Hold producers and others accountable when such expertise is not accessed in hiring for a regional production.

On the individual level, identify local collaborators:

- Pick a mentor and/or offer oneself as a mentor;

- Contribute to national data-gathering initiatives by completing your individual and organizational profiles on the national database;

- Identify resource-sharing opportunities and communicate those to regional and national networks;

- Advocate for other Latina/o theatermakers;

- Remember your roots as your star rises, and always list the Latina/o theatermakers and organizations that mentored your success within your official press and production biographies; and

- Hold institutions (and individuals) at all levels accountable for "culture poaching," the non-reciprocal exploitation of Latina/o creative labor and artistic production to enhance a non-Latina/o organization's reputation or bottom-line (often at the expense of community-based Latina/o arts organizations); call out culture poaching, and support those individuals and organizations who name the exploitation when it occurs.

ART-MAKING

On the national level, strategic initiatives include:

- Establish national networks of peer-review and mutual mentorship for artists, producers, and scholars;

- Build development programs for Latina/o designers, directors, and producers; and

- Gather data to configure a national touring network of campuses, companies, and venues interested in presenting Latina/o theater work.

On the regional and local levels:

- Establish skill-sharing and skill-enhancement groups, including grant workshops, portfolio reviews, and writing groups.

On the individual level:

- Share news of your work with other Latina/o theatermakers and support other Latina/o theatermakers by getting to know their work.

CONVENING/NETWORKING

On the national level, execute the two upcoming Convenings: Los Angeles *Encuentro* in 2014 and Chicago *Carnaval* in 2015. Begin funding Convenings further into the future:

- Develop national funding strategy to sustain national and regional convenings; and

- Prioritize the opportunity for regional/local and national leaders to develop mutually-productive relationships through the development of and participation in collaborative events.

On the regional and local level, create strategic partnerships:

- Establish regional Latina/o theater consortiums (like ALTA in Chicago and TANTO in Dallas); and

- Cultivate connections among local Latina/o theatermakers and allies by executing regional convenings, *encuentros*, or other skill-sharing ventures (Latina/o academic symposiums, actor audition showcases, and development workshops for small companies).

On the individual level, elevate your involvement:

- Participate in national and regional Convenings whenever possible; and

- Volunteer to serve on steering or advisory committees of your regional and/or national Convenings.

SCHOLARSHIP

Elevate targeted communications and academic relationships at the national level:

- Commission an ATHE white paper addressing best practices for diversification of university theater programs;

- Compile a list of university departments, faculty, and programs invested in integrating Latina/o theater materials into their curriculum and production seasons;

- Establish a task force to develop a plan for the Fornés Institute, which would offer itinerant workshops, permanent retreat/gathering space, and a library.

At the regional and local levels, leverage the resources of the university to:

- Cultivate mutually-beneficial partnerships (archival partnerships, productions, residencies, etc.) between particular campuses and individual Latina/o theatermakers;

- Create actual or virtual repositories of Latina/o theater materials of use to students at your campus and beyond;

- Create regional pipelines of emerging talent by establishing networks connecting Latina/o theater students and their allies (both student and faculty) at area campuses;

- Fortify generative connections and collaborations among artists and scholars across institutions and organizations; and

- Celebrate the publication of scholarly and other works about Latina/o theater with parties, readings, and other events that open the scholarship process to communities beyond academia.

Heighten the profile of Latina/o work:

- Integrate Latina/o theater (plays, productions, scholarship) into your curriculum at every appropriate opportunity;

- Submit to anthologies and Café Onda as regularly as possible; and

- Assist in the ongoing documentation of Latina/o theatermaking at all levels (community-based, educational, national, regional) by writing about it in a diversity of genres and publications.

At the conclusion of the Strategy session, the co-facilitators posed two particular tasks to those assembled.

Both tasks challenged the Convening participants to chart their commitment to the strategic work of the LTC beyond the Convening itself. First, Olga Sanchez challenged everyone to take a moment to call or text someone. "Tell them," Sanchez prompted. "Tell them 'I need to talk to you when I get back about something that came up at the LTC Convening.'" For the next several minutes, the room hummed with the sounds of voices following Sanchez's exhortation. Sanchez asked the group to contemplate the many strategic initiatives proposed by the Convening. As the group sat silently for a long moment, she asked, "Where do you think you could commit?" Clyde Valentín invited everyone to retrieve their *lotería* cards and write their names on the back of the cards. "Write down the one thing you are willing to do, moving forward. …Make a commitment to yourself that you are going to contribute to this movement the best way that you can." As the group members wrote out their commitments (placing a star next to their names if they wished to serve on the national Steering Committee of the LTC), the co-facilitators removed all the poster-sized pieces of paper containing the Strategy Group recommendations to reveal again the timeline hidden beneath.

"The timeline can once again be with us in the space as we close," Valentín concluded, "a reminder [that] culture is a continuum."

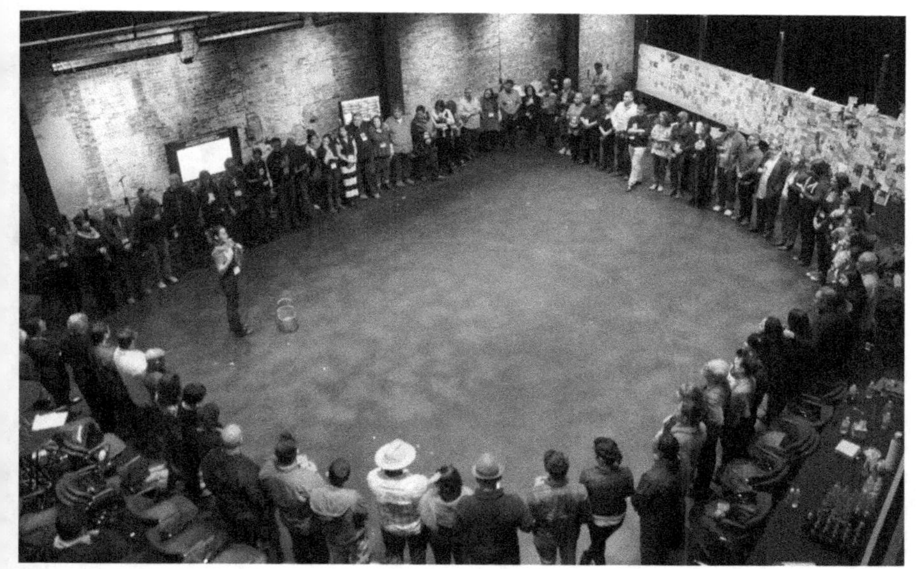

Closing the Circle

Kinan Valdez invited the group to "help us rec-
reate the ceremonial space that we started with."
Those assembled moved first to clear the center
of the space of chairs and other items and then
to form a final large circle around the perimeter.
"Please lift your *lotería* cards." Valdez invited everyone to breathe deeply. "Hold them close to
you." Reminding the group of their arrival from
each of the four directions, Valdez declared, "Now
that we are together, unified, we embrace the directions, as a full community, as a full *familia*."

Olga Sanchez stepped forward. "By way of
closing our circle, we ask you to, one at a time,
come forward and place your card in this basket,"
the gesture affirming the commitment written on

"Hey! This
is sacred.
Quit laughing."
—Clyde Valentín

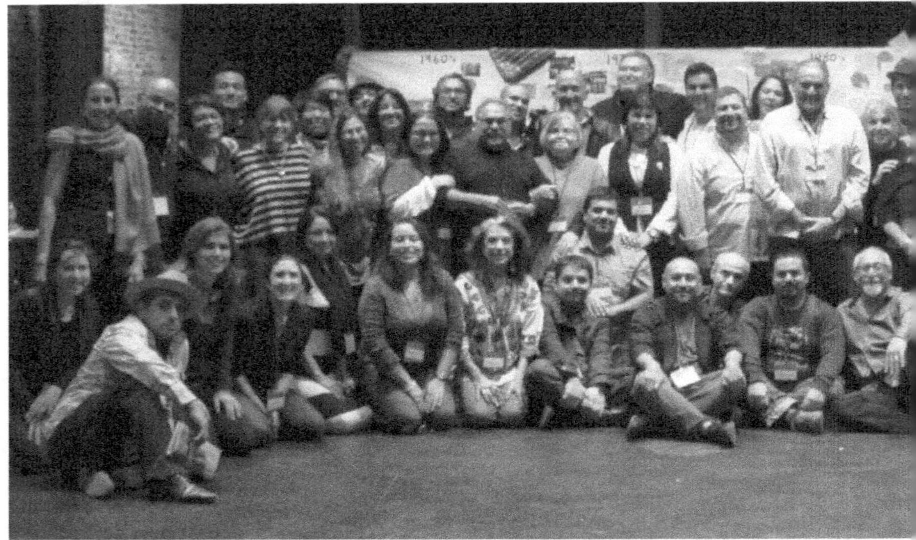

FIG. 25

the reverse of the card. Then, Sanchez instructed the group: "Once you've placed your card, go and pick up your item [from the altar] and come back to your place in the circle." Clyde Valentín then explained the closing ritual's final step, wherein each person was invited to give her or his altar offering to another Convening participant. After some confusion erupted regarding the rules of the "gift exchange," Valentín confirmed the simple prompt—give what you brought to someone—he wryly admonished the group, "Hey! This is sacred. Quit laughing."

Luis Valdez led the Convening's closing ceremony. He began with a parable—spoken first in Nahuatl, then in Spanish, finally in English—before leading, through his own action, the three steps of the closing ritual. And, one by one, each of those assembled followed in near silence, placing *lotería* cards in the basket, retrieving offerings from the

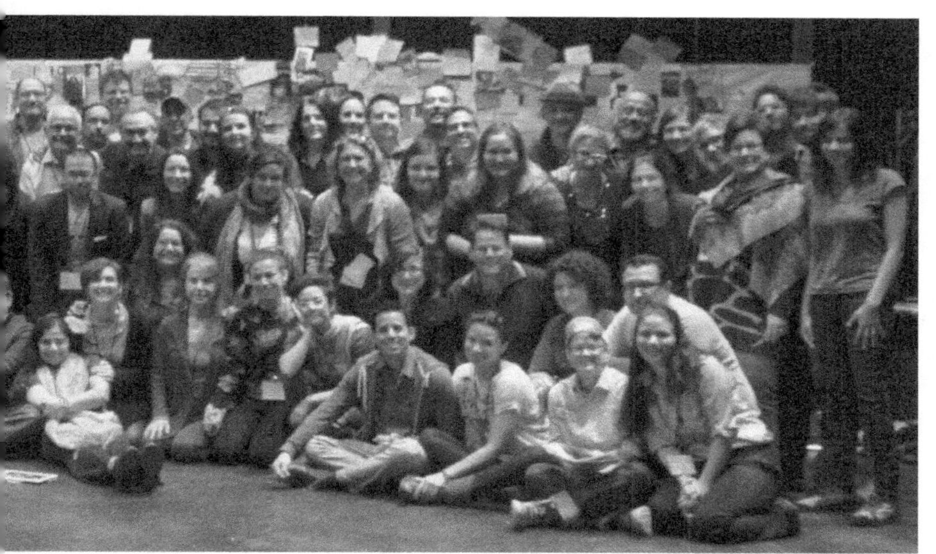

altar, and returning to the circle. Next, after a brief reminder of the protocols of the offering exchange, Olga Sanchez collected the basket, placed it on the altar, and turned to the group. "Ready? Go!" The group erupted in a bustle of activity, passing on their altar offerings and exchanging words and embraces.

Finally, Kinan Valdez invited everyone to form one circle. "We are here in the final moments of our Convening," Valdez affirmed. Valdez, Sanchez, and Valentín guided everyone first in a stomping round of appreciation for HowlRound, and then in an accelerating build of energy and a final rush toward the center to release the Convening's power to the world. Thus, with a resounding round of howling cheers, the 2013 LTC National Convening the came to its close.

List of Figures

Convening Participants

Christopher Acebo, *Oregon Shakespeare Festival**

Luis Alfaro, *Playwright**

Elisa Maria Alvarado, *Teatro Visión*

Juan Amador, *Campo Santo*

Kevin Becerra, *ArtsEmerson: The World on Stage**

Alexandria Maria Beech, *Playwright*

Rose Cano, *eSe Teatro*

José Carrasquillo, *Director*

Juliette Carrillo, *Director**

Marissa Chibas, *Duende CalArts*

Migdalia Cruz, *Playwright*

Christopher De Paola, *Playwright*

Sandra Delgado, *Collaboraction, Teatro Vista*

Georgina H. Escobar, *Playwright*

Micha Espinosa, *Arizona State University*

Evelina Fernandez, *Latino Theatre Company, Los Angeles Theater Center*

Olga Garay-English, *Executive Director, Los Angeles Department of Cultural Affairs*Δ

Anthony J. Garcia, *Su Teatro*

Lydia Garcia, *Oregon Shakespeare Festival*

Regina García, *Scenic Designer*

Amparo Garcia-Crow, *Independent Artist*

Anne García-Romero, *Playwright/Scholar, University of Notre Dame*[†‡]

Ricardo Gutierrez, *Teatro Vista*[△]

Brian Eugenio Herrera, *Princeton University*[△]

Jorge Huerta, *Professor Emeritus, University of California-San Diego*[△]

Sandra Islas, *Latino Producers Action Network*

Daniel Jáquez, *Director*

Alberto Justiano, *Teatro del Pueblo*

Abel López, *GALA Theatre*[*]

Melinda Lopez, *Huntington Theatre Playwright-in-Residence*

Tiffany Ana López, *University of California-Riverside*[△]

Josefina López, *CASA 0101 Theater*

Nancy García Loza, *Colectivo El Pozo*[△]

David Lozano, *Cara Mía Theatre Co.*

Sandra Marquez, *Teatro Vista, Northwestern University*

Teresa Marrero, *University of North Texas*

Irma Mayorga, *Playwright/Scholar, Dartmouth College*

Alexandra Meda, *Teatro Luna*

Noe Montez, *Tufts University*

Richard Montoya, *Culture Clash*

Lou Moreno, *INTAR Theatre*

Marcos Nájera, Actor, *Director, Journalist*

Matthew Paul Olmos, *Playwright*

Marisela Treviño Orta, *Playwright*

Jacob Padrón, *Steppenwolf Theatre Company*[*]

Richard Perez, *Chicago Dramatists, Hope College*[*]

Marc David Pinate, *Borderlands Theatre*

Lisa Portes, *DePaul University, Director*[*]

Rose Portillo, *About Productions*

Jesus A. Reyes, *East LA Rep*

Tlaloc Rivas, *Director, University of Iowa*[†]

Beatriz J. Rizk, *Teatro Avante, Scholar*

Anthony Rodriguez, *Aurora Theatre/Teatro del Sol**

Chantal Rodriguez, *Latino Theater Company, Los Angeles Theatre Center*△

Diane Rodriguez, *Center Theatre Group**

Elaine Romero, *Chicago Dramatists, Playwright*

Jerry Ruiz, *Director*

Mario Ernesto Sánchez, *Teatro Avante**

Olga Sanchez, *Milagro**□

Tanya Saracho, *Playwright*

Bernardo Solano, *Playwright, California State Polytechnic University*

Octavio Solis, *Playwright*△

Tony Sonera, *Badass Theatre Company*△

Caridad Svich, *NoPassport, Playwright*

Cándido Tirado, *Playwright*

Enrique Urueta, *Playwright*

Kinan Valdez, *El Teatro Campesino**‡□

Luis Valdez, *El Teatro Campesino*

Lupe Valdez, *El Teatro Campesino*

Mark Valdez, *Network of Ensemble Theaters (NET)*

Clyde Valentín, *HI-ARTS, Southern Methodist University**‡□

José Luis Valenzuela, *Latino Theater Company, Los Angeles Theatre Center**

Abigail Vega, *Teatro Luna*

Ivan Vega, *UrbanTheater Company*

Tiffany Vega, *HI-ARTS*

Laurie Woolery, *Director, Producer*

Patricia Ybarra, *Brown University**

Stephanie Ybarra, *The Public Theater*

Karen Zacarías, *Playwright**

Note: Affiliations listed reflect employment status as of October 31, 2013.

Group 1: Regional Theater

Christopher Acebo, Lydia Garcia, Melinda Lopez, Jacob Padron (moderator), Diane Rodriguez, Tanya Saracho, Stephanie Ybarra, and Karen Zacarías.

Group 2: Community-Based/Culturally-Specific

Elisa Marina Alvarado, Sandra Delgado, Tony Garcia (moderator), Ricardo Gutierrez, Alberto Justiano, Josefina López, Nancy García Loza, David Lozano, Sandra Marquez, Lou Moreno, Marcos Nájera, Anthony Rodriguez, Ivan Vega, and Tiffany Vega.

Group 3: Academia

Marissa Chibas, Micha Espinosa, Brian Herrera, Jorge Huerta, Tiffany Ana López, Teresa Marrero, Irma Mayorga, Noe Montez, Richard Perez, Beatriz Rizk, Bernardo Solano, and Patricia Ybarra (moderator).

Group 4: Independent Artists

José Carrasquillo, Christopher De Paola, Georgina H. Escobar, Amparo Garcia-Crow, Anne García-Romero (moderator), Matthew Paul Olmos, Rose Portillo, Elaine Romero, Tony Sonera, Cándido Tirado, and Enrique Urueta,

Group 5: Independent Artists

Luis Alfaro, Alexandra Maria Beech, Juliette Carrillo, Migdalia Cruz, Regina García, Marisela Treviño Orta, Lisa Portes (moderator), Tlaloc Rivas, Jerry Ruiz, Octavio Solis, and Laurie Woolery.

Group 6: International Work

Kevin Becerra, Rose Cano, Evelina Fernandez, Daniel Jáquez, Abel López, Alexandra Meda, Marc David Pinate, Mario Ernesto Sánchez (moderator), and Caridad Svich.

Group 7: Ensemble-Based Work

Juan Amador, Sandra Islas, Richard Montoya, Jesus Reyes, Chantal Rodriguez, Luis Valdez, Lupe Valdez, Mark Valdez, José Luis Valenzuela (moderator), and Abigail Vega.

CONOCIMIENTO 2: Wisdom Groups

Group 1: 6-10 years in the field

Alexandra Maria Beech, Georgina H. Escobar, Sandra Islas, Noe Montez, Marisela Treviño Orta, Jacob Padrón, Chantal Rodriguez, and Enrique Urueta (moderator).

Wisdom Group 2: 11-15 years in the field

Sandra Delgado, Lydia Garcia, Daniel Jáquez, Alexandra Meda, Matthew Paul Olmos, Jerry Ruiz, Tanya Saracho (moderator), Ivan Vega, and Stephanie Ybarra.

Wisdom Group 3: 16-20 years in the field

Christopher Acebo (moderator), Juan Amador, Christopher De Paola, Regina García Anne García-Romero, David Lozano, Marcos Nájera, Marc David Pinate, Patricia Ybarra, and Karen Zacarías.

Wisdom Group 4: 21-25 years in the field

José Carrasquillo, Alberto Justiano, Sandra Marquez, Teresa Marrero, Jesus Reyes, Anthony Rodriguez (moderator), Elaine Romero, Caridad Svich, and Tiffany Vega.

Wisdom Group 5: 21-25 years in the field

Juliette Carrillo, Micha Espinosa, Brian Herrera, Tiffany Ana López, Lou Moreno (moderator), Lisa Portes, Tlaloc Rivas, Mark Valdez, and Laurie Woolery.

Wisdom Group 6: 26-30 years in the field
Luis Alfaro, Migdalia Cruz, Amparo Garcia-Crow, Josefina López, Irma Mayorga, Richard Montoya, Richard Perez, and Tony Sonera (moderator).

Wisdom Group 7: 31-35 years in the field*
Rose Cano, Marissa Chibas, Evelina Fernandez, Abel López, Beatriz Rizk, Bernardo Solano, Octavio Solis (moderator),Cándido Tirado, and Abigail Vega.*

Wisdom Group 8: 35+ years in the field*
Elisa Marina Alvarado, Kevin Becerra,* Olga Garay-English, Tony Garcia, Ricardo Gutierrez, Jorge Huerta (moderator), Nancy García Loza,* Rose Portillo, Diane Rodriguez, Mario Ernesto Sánchez, Luis Valdez, Lupe Valdez, and José Luis Valenzuela.

* Wisdom Groups 7 and 8 also included those Convening participants with less than five years in the field.

CONOCIMIENTO 3: Strategy Groups
Note: some Convening participants floated from group to group. Only those who were attributed quotes in notes are listed here.

Group 1: Scholarship
Migdalia Cruz, Jorge Huerta (co-moderator),Teresa Marrero, Irma Mayorga, Noe Montez, Beatriz Rizk, Enrique Urueta, and Patricia Ybarra (co-moderator).

Group 2: Art-Making
Luis Alfaro, Juliette Carrillo (moderator), Josefina López, Jesus Reyes, Luis Valdez, Lupe Valdez, and Laurie Woolery.

Group 3: Café Onda

Georgina H. Escobar, Brian Herrera, Marisela Treviño Orta, Lydia Garcia, Nancy García Loza, Tlaloc Rivas (moderator), Elaine Romero, and Octavio Solis.

Group 4: Festivals

Olga Garay-English, Chantal Rodriguez (moderator), Lisa Portes, and José Luis Valenzuela.

Group 5: Advocacy

Elisa Marina Alvarado, Juan Amador, Abel López (moderator), Melinda Lopez, David Lozano, Mario Ernesto Sánchez, Olga Sanchez, and Tiffany Vega.

Group 6: Networking

José Carrasquillo, Regina García, Sandra Islas, Alberto Justiano, Jacob Padrón, Richard Perez (moderator), Diane Rodriguez, Cándido Tirado, and Stephanie Ybarra.

Group 7: Convening

Sandra Delgado, Amparo Garcia-Crow, Sandra Marquez, and Mark Valdez (moderator).

Group 8: Mentorship

Tiffany Ana López (moderator), Lou Moreno, Marcos Nájera, Bernardo Solano, Abigail Vega, and Karen Zacarías.

Resources Derived
from the Wisdom Groups

The following is a compilation of most of the resources brainstormed among the participants at the eight Wisdom Groups that met during the final day of the Convening. This listing is by no means comprehensive, but rather deeply idiosyncratic, leaving as many gaps as it fills. Indeed, this listing might be best considered a provisional draft of a much-needed catalogue of the many festivals, networks, organizations, and resources built by and serving Latina/o theater artists since 1986.

ACADEMIC ORGANIZATIONS

- American Alliance for Theatre & Education (AATE): dedicated to theatre for youth in schools and communities.

- American Society for Theatre Research (ASTR): a United States-based professional organization that fosters scholarship on worldwide theater and performance, both historical and contemporary.

- Association for Theatre in Higher Education (ATHE): an intellectual and artistic center for producing new knowledge about theater and performance-related disciplines and an advocate for the field of theater and performance in higher education.

- Hemispheric Institute for Performance & Politics (HEMI): a collaborative, multilingual, and interdisciplinary consortium of activists, artists, institutions, and scholars throughout the Americas.

- University Resident Theatre Association (URTA): the nation's oldest and largest consortium of theater training programs and partnered professional theater companies.

- Voice and Speech Trainers Association (VASTA): organization dedicated to serving the needs of the voice and speech profession and to developing the art and science of the human voice.

ARTS LEADERSHIP ORGANIZATIONS & INITIATIVES

- Americans for the Arts Action Fund

- Grantmakers in the Arts (GIA)

- National Association of Latino Arts and Cultures (NALAC)

- National Performance Network (NPN)

- Network of Ensemble Theaters (NET)

- Theatre Communications Group (TCG)

DIGITAL PLATFORMS/NETWORKS

- 2AMt (a gathering place for theater ideas): 2amtheatre.com

- American Theatre Archive Project (ATAP): americantheatrearchiveproject.org

- Café Onda: cafeonda.com

- Contemporary Performance Network (CPN): contemporaryperformance.org

- Cuban Digital Theater Archive (CDTA): cubantheater.org

- HEMI Archive: hemi.nyu.edu/eng/archive

- LATC Newsletter: thelatc.org/about/latino-theater-company

- ATHE's Latina/o Focus Group (LFG):
  sites.google.com/site/latinofocusgroup

- New Mexican Playwrights: newmexicodramatists.org

- NoPassport: nopassport.org

- TCG 2.0 (Year Round Conference Community): tcg.pathable.com

FESTIVALS

- Latino New Play Festival, Austin, TX (2011-)

- Brown and Out, Casa 0101, East Los Angeles, CA (2011-)

- *Celebración Artística de las Américas* (CALA) Festival, Phoenix, AZ
  (2011- alternating years)

- *Chingona* Fest, McAllen, TX (2012, 2013)

- Crossing Borders Festival, Two River Theater, Red Bank, NJ (2010-)

- FronteraFest, Hyde Park Theatre and ScriptWorks, Austin, TX
  (1996-)

- Latino Theater Festival, Goodman Theatre, Chicago, IL (2008-)

- *Hecho en Califas Festival,* La Pena Cultural Center, Berkeley, CA
  (2000-20101)

- Ignition Festival of New Plays, Victory Gardens Theater,
  Chicago, IL (2011-)

- IOne Minute Play Festival, INTAR, New York, NY (2012-)

- International Hispanic Theatre Festival, Teatro Avante, Miami, FL
  (1986-)

- Latino MixFest, Atlantic Theatre, New York, NY (2010-)

- Live Action Exchange (LAX) Festival, Los Angeles Performance
  Practice and the Bootleg Theater, Los Angeles, CA (2013-)

- LIFT (Latino International Theatre Festival of New York
  aka TeatroStageFest) New York, NY (2005-)

- La Luna Nueva Festival, Miracle Theatre, Portland, OR (2009-)

- The Ñ Series, The Ñ Project, Chicago, IL (2010-2012)

- NET Microfests, diverse sites nationally (2010-)

- New York International Latino Theatre Festival, The Public Theater,
  New York, NY (1976-1991)

- 30/30, Gun Control Theatre Action, Spark, NoPassport, New York
  City and diverse sites internationally (2012-)

- The One Festival, Teatro Latea, Brooklyn, NY (2006-)

- Political Theatre Festival, Teatro del Pueblo, Minneapolis-St.Paul,
  MN (2002-)

- Radar LA, CTG, Public Theater and REDCAT, Los Angeles, CA
  (2011-)

- Revolutions International Theatre Festival, Tricklock Company,
  Albuquerque, NM (1999-)

- Represent! A Multicultural Playwrights' Festival, The Hansberry
  Project, eSe Teatro, SIS Productions, and Pratidhwani, Seattle, WA
  (2011-)

- Tapas a la Teatro Vista Play Reading Series, Teatro Vista, Chicago,
  IL (2004-)

- International Festival of Hispanic Theater, Teatro de la Luna Arling-
  ton, VA (1998-)

- Teatro del Mundo International Theatre Festival, Teatro Dallas, Dallas, TX (1993-)

- Yo Solo Festival, Teatro Vista, Chicago, IL (2012)

DEVELOPMENT OPPORTUNITIES FOR LATINA/O ARTISTS

- 5/5/5 Initiative, Teatro Luna, diverse sites nationally

- FAIR Programs, Oregon Shakespeare Festival, Ashland, OR

- Fox Foundation Resident Actor Fellowships, Theatre Communications Group, New York, NY

- Late Night Teatro Vista, Teatro Vista, Chicago, IL

- Northwest Regional Latino Theatre Auditions, Seattle, WA and Portland, OR

- Mobile Shakespeare Unit, The Public Theater, New York, NY

- Shakespeare Dramaturgy Fellowship, Oregon Shakespeare Festival, Ashland, OR

- Unit52, INTAR, New York City, NY

LATINA/O PLAYWRIGHT DEVELOPMENT

- Emerging Writer's Group, The Public Theater, New York, NY: (2008- in alternate years)

- Writers in Residence Program, Hedgebrook, Whidbey Island, WA (1988-)

- Hispanic Playwrights-in-Residence Laboratory, INTAR, New York, NY (1981-), New York City, NY (1978-1991)

- Hispanic Playwrights Project, South Coast Repertory, Costa Mesa, CA (1986-2004)

* U.S./México Playwright Exchange Program, Lark Play Development Center, New York, NY (2006-)

* The Latino Theatre Initiative (LTI), Mark Taper Forum, Los Angeles, CA (1992-2005)

* Latina/o Plays Project (LPP), Oregon Shakespeare Festival, Ashland, OR 2013- (in alternate years)

* National Latino Playwriting Award, Arizona Theatre Company, Tucson, AZ (1995-

* Rolling World Premieres, National New Play Network (NNPN), diverse sites nationally (1998-)

* New Play Summit, Denver Center Theatre Company, Denver, CO (2006-)

* Black and Latino Playwrights Conference, Texas State University, San Marcos, TX (2003-)

* XX Playlab at Boston Center for the Arts, Company One Theatre, Boston, MA (2012-)

REGIONAL ALLIANCES

CALIFORNIA

* Bay Area Latino Theatre Artists Network (BALTAN) (2013-) facebook.com/pages/Bay-Area-Latino-Theatre-Artists-Network

* Latino Theatre Alliance Los Angeles (LTA/LA) (2012-) ltala.org

ILLINOIS

* Alliance of Latino Theatre Artists of Chicago (ALTA) (2011-) altachicago.org ,

NEW MEXICO

- *Colectivo Teatral Nuevo Mexico* (2014-) colectivoteatralnm.org

NEW YORK

- Alliance de Teatros Latinos Nueva York (2010-)

TEXAS

- Austin Latino Theater Alliance (ALTA) (2011-) altateatro.com

- Teatro Alianza of North Texas Organizations (TANTO) (2012-) tantoteatro.org

- San Antonio Latino Theater Alliance (SALTA) (2013-) facebook. com/SALTASanAntonio

NON-LATINA/O PRESENTERS WITH DEMONSTRATED COMMITMENT TO LATINA/O WORK

- Mixed Blood Theatre Company, Minneapolis, MN

- LAByrinth Theatre Company, New York, NY

- Page to Stage, The Kennedy Center, Washington D.C.

PUBLICATIONS

- Ollantay Theater Magazine (1993-) ollantaycenterforthearts.org

- Arte Publico Press (1979-) artepublicopress.com

Luis Valdez's Proposition:
A Theater for the New America(n)s

During the final strategy session, Luis Valdez questioned the strategic utility of the term "Latina/o" in the long-term. His intervention immediately elicited a surge of responses, both in Boston and on twitter.

> *When cars first came out they called them horseless carriages. …I think the Latina/o term will eventually phase itself out, because it's too limiting. And it is not going to give us the kind of support that we need, because it is ethnic. It is divisive ultimately. Really what are we about? What are we reflecting? I think what we are reflecting are the "New Americans"—who are we? We are the New American theater! Why not take it? We are not divorcing ourselves from it. We are providing a new beginning for the new American theater. We are the theater of New America—theater, by, for and about the New Americans.*

Just before the closing session, Valdez clarified that he wanted to affirm "the new American theater has to be a theater of new Americans and of the Americas." This constellation of notions continued to flow as the convening came to its close.

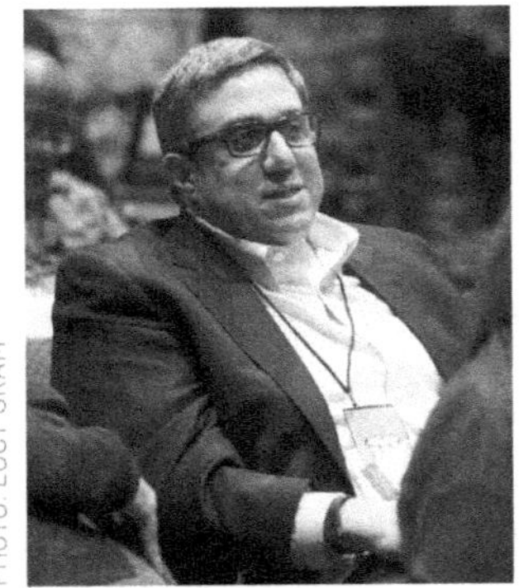

About the Author

Brian Eugenio Herrera is, by turns, a writer, teacher, scholar, and performer—presently based in New Jersey, but forever rooted in New Mexico. Herrera's work, both academic and creative, examines the history of gender, sexuality, and race within and through United States popular performance. He holds degrees from Brown University, the University of New Mexico, and Yale University, where he earned his PhD in American Studies. From 2007 to 2012, Herrera taught undergraduate and graduate courses in World Theatre History and Performance Theory in the Department of Theatre and Dance at the University of New Mexico, where he was recognized four times by The Project For New Mexico Graduates of Color as an Outstanding Faculty Member. In 2012, Herrera joined the faculty of Princeton University as Assistant Professor of Theater in the Lewis Center for the Arts. Herrera's first book, *Latin Numbers: Playing Latino in Twentieth Century U.S. Popular Performance*, is forthcoming from University of Michigan Press in the summer of 2015.

www.ingramcontent.com/pod-product-compliance
Lightning Source LLC
Chambersburg PA
CBHW050941050726
47592CB00007B/2392